3 STUDY GUIDES ON LENIN'S WRITINGS

3 Study Guides on Lenin's Writings

1 Class forces and strategy in the Russian Revolution
1902–17

2 Lenin's Struggle for a Revolutionary International
1907–16

3 Soviet Power and the Communist International
1918–19

PATHFINDER
New York London Montreal Sydney

ISBN 978-1-60488-073-1
Library of Congress Control Number 2016935339

Manufactured in the United States of America

First edition, 2017
Fourth printing, 2024

COVER DESIGN: Carole Caron

COVER PHOTO: Delegates to the Second Congress of the Communist International, Petrograd, July 1920, during a lunch break. In foreground, from left: *Karl Radek* (Soviet Russia); *Nikolai Bukharin* (Soviet Russia); *Mikhail Lashevich* (in uniform, Soviet Russia); *V.I. Lenin* (Soviet Russia); author *Maxim Gorky*; *Sergei Zorin* (wearing hat, Soviet Russia); *Gregory Zinoviev*, (Soviet Russia); *Charles Shipman*, US journalist, founding member of Mexican Communist party; *M.N. Roy*, founding member of Mexican and Indian Communist Parties.

PATHFINDER
www.pathfinderpress.com
Email: pathfinder@pathfinderpress.com

CONTENTS

PUBLISHER'S NOTE

These three study guides were prepared for weekly classes organized in the 1980s by branches of the Socialist Workers Party. Originally published as separate pamphlets, they are presented here in a single collection.

The first guide reviews Bolshevik leader V.I. Lenin's political strategy for the Russian Revolution—the course that guided the Bolshevik Party as it led workers and peasants to take power in October 1917.

The second takes up the Bolsheviks' struggle during the years prior to the revolution to help build a revolutionary working-class movement worldwide.

The third examines how the Bolsheviks used the power of the victorious workers state and the impulse the revolution gave to working-class struggles everywhere to build a new, Communist International.

The final item, by Bolshevik and Communist International leader Gregory Zinoviev, reviews the Marxist approach to wars from the battle to unify Italy in 1859 to the eve of the first imperialist world war in 1914.

Several books cited in this collection have been printed in multiple editions, for which pagination may vary. For titles from Pathfinder, the page numbers are for printings current with this 2017 reissue of the study guides.

—APRIL 2017

Class Forces and Strategy in Making the Russian Revolution (1902-1917)

Lenin's conception of the class forces and strategy in making the Russian revolution (1902–1917)

THIS READING LIST, based on one first compiled in 1982, is a guide to the study of Lenin's political strategy for the Russian revolution. This strategy, which determined both the political and organizational character of the Bolshevik Party, was the one around which that party was constructed and along which the Russian workers and peasants came to power in October 1917.

Several readings not included in the 1982 reading list have been added. All the items are by Lenin, and they can be found in various places in the books of his works put out by Moscow's Progress Publishers, as well as in volumes of Pathfinder's series The Communist International in Lenin's Time. Where the articles are available in more than one place, the list includes multiple references. Lenin's *Collected Works* are noted by the letters *CW;* the three-volume *Selected Works* by *SW;* and the Progress collection of Lenin on the *Alliance of the Working Class and Peasantry* by *AWCP.* Pathfinder's *Lenin's Struggle for a Revolutionary International* is noted by *LSRI; The German Revolution and the Debate on Soviet Power* by *GR;* and *Founding the Com-*

munist International by *FCI*.

Of course, this is only a very partial list of some of the most important articles, speeches, pamphlets, and resolutions relating to the question of the character of the Russian revolution and the class forces in it. Readers will find other Lenin writings that they may choose to add as reading for their class series.

The readings are listed in chronological order with a single exception—the first one. The initial item, an excerpt from *The Proletarian Revolution and the Renegade Kautsky,* provides a good overall review of the Bolsheviks' conception of the Russian revolution from 1902 to 1918, when Lenin wrote this polemic. In this article, Lenin reviews and defends his 1905 pamphlet, *Two Tactics of Social Democracy in the Democratic Revolution,* answering the centrist Karl Kautsky's attack on the October revolution for going beyond the bounds of bourgeois democracy.

"The question which Kautsky has so tangled up," Lenin writes, "was fully explained by the Bolsheviks as far back as 1905." He then goes on to explain the political conception, which runs like a thread through all the readings in this list:

> Things have turned out just as we said they would. The course taken by the revolution has confirmed the correctness of our reasoning.
>
> *First,* with the "whole" of the peasants against the monarchy, against the landowners, against medievalism (and to that extent the revolution remains bourgeois, bourgeois democratic).
>
> *Then,* with the poor peasants, with the semi-pro-

> letarians, with all the exploited, *against capitalism,* including the rural rich, the kulaks, the profiteers, and to that extent the revolution becomes a *socialist* one.
>
> To attempt to raise an artificial Chinese Wall between the first and the second, to separate them *by anything else* than the degree of preparedness of the proletariat and the degree of its unity with the poor peasants, means to distort Marxism dreadfully, to vulgarise it, to substitute liberalism in its place.

With this exception, however, the other articles are listed chronologically. This will enable you to follow the development of the proletarian program as part and parcel of the Leninist strategy of the Bolsheviks, the fundamental continuity of Bolshevism over two decades from 1902 to Lenin's death, and its concrete application to new conjunctures in the class struggle.

Steve Clark

Readings

The Proletarian Revolution and the Renegade Kautsky

(November 1918)

The section "Subservience to the Bourgeoisie in the Guise of Economic Analysis."

- In pamphlet form, pages 69–93.
- *CW* Volume 28, pages 295–319.
- *SW* Volume 3, pages 70–91.
- *GR,* pages 508–38 (2013 printing).

What Is To Be Done?

(February 1902)

The section "The Working Class as Vanguard Fighter for Democracy."

- Available in pamphlet form and many anthologies.
- *CW* Volume 5, pages 421–36.
- *SW* Volume 1, pages 152–65.

To the Rural Poor

(March 1903)

Sections 6 and 7.

- *CW* Volume 6, pages 406–30.
- *AWCP,* pages 69–97.

A Revolution of the 1789 or 1848 Type?

(March–April 1905)

- *CW* Volume 8, pages 257–59.

Draft Resolution on the Participation of the Social Democrats in a Provisional Revolutionary Government
(April 1905)

Sections 11–15.

- *CW* Volume 8, pages 379–99.

On the Provisional Revolutionary Government
(May 1905)

- *CW* Volume 8, pages 461–81.

The Democratic Tasks of the Revolutionary Proletariat
(June 1905)

- *CW* Volume 8, pages 511–18.

Sketch of a Provisional Revolutionary Government
(June–July 1905)

- *CW* Volume 8, pages 534–36.

Three Constitutions or Three Systems of Government
(June–July 1905)

- *CW* Volume 8, pages 557–59.

The Revolutionary Army and the Revolutionary Government
(July 1905)

- *CW* Volume 8, pages 560–68.

The Paris Commune and the Tasks of the Democratic Dictatorship
(July 1905)

• *On the Paris Commune,* Lenin, Progress Publishers, pages 114–20.

Two Tactics of Social Democracy in the Democratic Revolution
(June–July 1905)

- *CW* Volume 9, pages 15–140.
- *SW* Volume 1, pages 425–527.
- Also available in pamphlet form.

Social Democracy's Attitude Toward the Peasant Movement
(September 1905)

- *CW* Volume 9, pages 230–39.
- *AWCP,* pages 121–31.

Petty-Bourgeois and Proletarian Socialism
(November 1905)

- *CW* Volume 9, pages 438–46.
- *AWCP,* pages 132–41.

Our Tasks and the Soviet of Workers' Deputies
(November 1905)

- *CW* Volume 10, pages 17–28.

The Proletariat and the Peasantry
(November 1905)

- *CW* Volume 10, pages 40–43.
- *AWCP,* pages 142–46.

Preface to the Russian Translation of K. Kautsky's Pamphlet 'The Driving Forces and Prospects of the Russian Revolution'

(December 1906)

- *CW* Volume 11, pages 408–13.

The Agrarian Question and the Forces of the Revolution
(April 1907)

- *CW* Volume 12, pages 333–36.
- *AWCP,* pages 175–79.

The Agrarian Programme of Social Democracy in the First Russian Revolution, 1905–1907
"Conclusion" (Nov.–Dec. 1907)

- *CW* Volume 13, pages 421–29.
- *AWCP,* pages 180–89.

The Assessment of the Russian Revolution
(April 1908)

- *CW* Volume 15, pages 50–62.

The Aim of the Proletarian Struggle in Our Revolution
(March 1909)

- *CW* Volume 15, pages 360–79.

The Defeat of Russia and the Revolutionary Crisis
(September 1915)

- *CW* Volume 21, pages 378–82.
- *LSRI,* pages 415–19 (2014 printing).

Several Theses
(October 1915)

- *CW* Volume 21, pages 401–4.

- *LSRI,* pages 592–96.

On the Two Lines in the Revolution
(November 1915)

- *CW* Volume 21, pages 415–20.
- *LSRI,* pages 586–90.

Lecture on the 1905 Revolution
(January 1917)

- *CW* Volume 23, pages 236–53.

Letters from Afar
(March 1917)

- *CW* Volume 23, pages 295–342.
- Also available in pamphlet form.

The Tasks of the Proletariat in the Present Revolution [The April Theses]
(April 1917)

- *CW* Volume 24, pages 19–26.
- *SW* Volume 2, pages 29–33.

The Dual Power
(April 1917)

- *CW* Volume 24, pages 38–41.
- *SW* Volume 2, pages 34–36.

Letter on Tactics
(April 1917)

- *CW* Volume 24, pages 42–54.

The Tasks of the Proletariat in Our Revolution: Draft Platform for the Proletarian Party

(April 1917)

- *CW* Volume 24, pages 55–91.
- *SW* Volume 2, pages 37–65.

From a Publicist's Diary [Peasants and Workers]
(September 1917)

- *CW* Volume 25, pages 278–86.
- *AWCP,* pages 221–30.

Postscript to 'The Agrarian Programme of Social Democracy. . . .'
(September 1917)

- *CW* Volume 13, pages 430–31.

Report on Land
(October 1917)

- *CW* Volume 26, pages 257–61.
- *AWCP,* pages 231–36.

The Third International and Its Place in History
(April 1919)

- *CW* Volume 29, pages 305–13.
- *FCI,* pages 51–60 (2015 printing).

A Contribution to the History of the Dictatorship Question
(October 1920)

- *CW* Volume 31, pages 340–61.

The Fourth Anniversary of the October Revolution
(October 1921)

- *CW* Volume 33, pages 51–59.
- *SW* Volume 3, pages 579–86.

Our Revolution
(January 1923)

- *CW* Volume 33, pages 476–80.
- *SW* Volume 3, pages 705–8.
- *Marx, Engels, Marxism,* Progress Publishers, pages 453–56.

Lenin's Struggle for a Revolutionary International

Study Guide for 'Lenin's Struggle for a Revolutionary International'

THIS READING LIST is a guide to a study of the documents on ten years of Bolshevik struggle for a revolutionary international working-class movement. It is based primarily on *Lenin's Struggle for a Revolutionary International*, the first volume in the Pathfinder series, The Communist International in Lenin's Time.

The reading list contains the most important material in *Lenin's Struggle for a Revolutionary International*, together with the background commentary that introduces each document in that book. Page numbers have been chosen to include the commentary. All page references refer to this collection, except when other books are indicated.

Lenin's Struggle for a Revolutionary International is organized into chapters on different topics and periods. Thus, a fuller picture of the political questions covered by this reading list can be gained by reading additional material from the chapters from which the bulk of the materials in a particular section are taken. This outline is based on the party's experience with the two Lenin study guides. Branches that decide to do this series will develop their own plan for the pace at which this material will be read and discussed, as they are doing with the other Lenin classes. The aim of the study guide is to present the readings in a coherent way that will help comrades organize themselves through their branches to get the most out of these classes.

Part 1: A general overview

The best general introduction to the political themes discussed in this study guide is the pamphlet *Socialism and War* by V.I. Lenin and Gregory Zinoviev. This was distributed as a presentation of the Bolshevik point of view to all the delegates at the September 1915 Zimmerwald Conference, and it became a widely circulated statement of the revolutionary proletarian position during the first imperialist world war.

It is recommended that each branch begin this class series by spending a number of weeks discussing this pamphlet. Only excerpts from this pamphlet appear in *Lenin's Struggle for a Revolutionary International.* Comrades can read the full text, however, in volume 21, pages 295–338 of Lenin's *Collected Works,* or by obtaining the Moscow edition of *Socialism and War* as a separate pamphlet.

Socialism and War contains a number of historical references and political ideas that may be unfamiliar to many comrades. It is not necessary to try to clarify and figure them all out in these opening sessions of the class series, however, since all the major themes and background material will be treated in greater detail in the later readings. Subsequent sections of the study guide will refer back to relevant excerpts from *Socialism and*

War. After branches have completed this study guide, they may want to go back and do one or two sessions on *Socialism and War* once again as a summary and conclusion to the series.

As part of the general introduction to the class series, the introduction to *Lenin's Struggle for a Revolutionary International*, pages 11–28, should also be read; a class session could be set aside for discussion of it early in the series.

Supplementary reading:
Comrades may find it useful to read Zinoviev's article, "Wars: Defensive and Aggressive," which is appended to this study guide. Written in collaboration with Lenin at about the same time as *Socialism and War*, it reviews the Marxist approach to wars in the light of historical experiences from the Italian war of 1859 to the eve of the First World War.

Part 2: The rise of imperialism and the crisis of the Second International

Discussions on this section of the study guide will be aided by a review of Chapter 1 of *Socialism and War*, pages 9–27 of the pamphlet edition, or pages 299–316 of volume 21 of the *Collected Works*. Comrades should also read Farrell Dobbs, *Revolutionary Continuity*, volume 1, pages 165–74 (2009 printing).

The Stuttgart Congress of 1907

The Second International's clearest discussion on the issues posed by the rise of imperialism took place at its 1907 Stuttgart congress, which opened a new stage in the efforts by the Bolsheviks to draw around them an international revolutionary Marxist current. Suggested readings are:

- Lenin, "The International Socialist Congress at Stuttgart," pages 80–90.
- The Colonialism Debate at Stuttgart, pages 32–50.
- The Immigration Commission, pages 51–57. (See also the first full paragraph on page 519 from Lenin's 1915 "Letter to the Secretary of the Socialist Propaganda League.")
- War and Militarism, pages 58–80.
- Zinoviev, "The Tendency Struggle at the Stuttgart Congress," pages 90–97.

The fight against opportunism in Germany, 1907–14

In the years following the Stuttgart conference, the debates that occurred there continued throughout the Second International. The conflicts were particularly sharp in the German party, which was the largest organization in the International and the one with the greatest political authority. An overview of the political degeneration of the German Social Democracy was presented by Zinoviev in his 1916 article, "The Social Roots of Opportunism." This section of the study guide should open with reading excerpts from that article on pages 703–21. Other readings are:

- 1907 Reichstag Debate on the Military Budget, pages 101–8.
- Lenin, "Two Worlds," pages 118–23. This 1910 article not only presents Lenin's views at that time of the state of the evolution of the German SPD, but also points to the pressures on workers' parties in imperialist countries toward parliamentary cretinism and other forms of class collaboration during periods of relative bourgeois legality

and economic stability, when no pre-revolutionary or revolutionary situation is on the agenda.

- The Molkenbuhr Letter on Morocco, pages 132–37.
- The SPD's 1913 Declaration on Taxes for War, pages 158–67.

Toward the collapse of the Second International

- The Balkan Wars and the Basel Congress Manifesto, pages 146–58.
- Zinoviev, "Legacy of the Second International," pages 176–80.

Part 3: Revolutionary policy against imperialist war

These readings cover the betrayal in August 1914 by the opportunist leaders of the SPD and the Second International; the revolutionary internationalist stand of Lenin and the Bolshevik Party; the position of other revolutionists such as Leon Trotsky and Karl Liebknecht; and the chauvinist response of German centrist leader Karl Kautsky. Background material to this section will be found in Farrell Dobbs, *Revolutionary Continuity*, volume 1, "The Supreme Test of War," pages 174–79. It can also be useful to review the sections of *Socialism and War* from pages 16–27 and pages 35–42 (pages 306–16 and pages 323–30 in volume 21 of the *Collected Works*).

Collapse of the Second International

- Background on the outbreak of war, pages 183–85.
- Two Resolutions Adopted by the International Socialist Bureau, page 191.

- Betrayal by the SPD Opportunist Leadership, pages 193–203.
- Lenin, "The Tasks of Revolutionary Social-Democracy in the War," pages 219–23.

Supplementary reading:

- July 1914 Session of the ISB, pages 185–91; The working class in Russia and the war, pages 205–15.

National defense or social revolution

- Lenin, "The War and Russian Social-Democracy," pages 248–57.
- Lenin, "The Position and Tasks of the Socialist International," pages 257–61.
- Kautsky, "Internationalism and the War," pages 231–38.
- Liebknecht, "Explanation of War Credits Vote," pages 274–78, and "The Main Enemy is At Home," pages 278–80.
- Trotsky, "War and the International," pages 238–48.
- Lenin, "The Defeat of One's Own Government in the Imperialist War," pages 261–70.
- Trotsky, "Defeat and Revolution," pages 270–74.
- Lenin, "The Collapse of the Second International," pages 316 (paragraph 2)–329.

Debate with Kautsky on imperialism

Following the outbreak of World War I, the theoretical positions that had been developed by German SPD leader Karl Kautsky about the nature of modem imperialism were used by many centrists to justify their adaptation to social chauvinism and the war policies of the exploiters in their own countries. Below is an excerpt from Kautsky's main article on this subject, written just prior to the outbreak of the war, along with Lenin's political response to these views in light of the subsequent capitulation of the social chauvinists and centrists.

- Kautsky, "Imperialism," pages 284–87.
- Lenin, excerpt from "The Social Chauvinists' Sophisms," pages 329–30.
- Lenin, "The Collapse of the Second International," pages 223–32 in volume 21 of the *Collected Works* (an excerpt from this passage can be found in *Lenin s Struggle for a Revolutionary International*, pages 310–14).

Supplementary reading:

- Käte Duncker, "The Economic Causes of the War," pages 287–89.

Part 4: Launching the struggle for a new international

The Bolsheviks responded to the political collapse of the Second International by launching the fight for a new International, cleansed of opportunism, chauvinism, and centrism. In late 1915 they formed the Zimmerwald Left, the first ongoing international grouping of revolutionary Marxists in Lenin's time. It was the immediate precursor to the Communist International. At the September 1915 Zimmerwald Conference, this minority revolutionary current clashed politically with the hesitant positions of the centrist and left-centrist currents there.

Background to this section of the study guide can be

found in Farrell Dobbs, *Revolutionary Continuity*, volume 2, pages 78–86 (2009 printing). The other readings are:

- Preparing the Zimmerwald Conference, pages 430–36.
- Liebknecht, "Letter to the Zimmerwald Conference," pages 439–41.
- Radek's report on behalf of the Zimmerwald Left; Zimmerwald Left Draft Resolution and Manifesto, pages 452–60.
- Zimmerwald Conference Debate: Ledebour; Lenin; Trotsky, pages 460–67.
- Zimmerwald Left Statement, page 480–81.
- Zimmerwald Manifesto, pages 485–90.
- Lenin, "The First Step," pages 499–506.

Supplementary reading:

- Trotsky, "The Work of the Zimmerwald Conference," pages 495–99; Radek, "The Zimmerwald Left," pages 506–15.

The ultimate outcome to Lenin's efforts to influence and win these currents, however, was still unresolved prior to the outbreak of the Russian revolution. The readings below deal with the political evolution of these currents and their relationships with the Bolsheviks between 1914 and 1917.

The Spartacist current in Germany

Branches should read the background material on Rosa Luxemburg and the Spartacist current in Germany in Dobbs, *Revolutionary Continuity*, volume 2, pages 40–44 and 71–76. Material from Dobbs on Anton Pannekoek and the ultraleftist current influenced by him can be found on pages

44–52 of that same volume.

- Liebknecht, "War and Education," pages 664–66.
- Luxemburg, "Theses on the Tasks of Social-Democracy," pages 615–22.
- Luxemburg, "Three Resolutions of Internationale Group," pages 667–72.
- Luxemburg, "The Crisis in the German Social Democracy," pages 628–46.
- Lenin, "On the Junius Pamphlet," pages 647–50 and pages 656–63. (The section on self-determination, pages 650–56, is contained in Section 5 of this study guide.)

Supplementary reading:

- Liebknecht, "Statement to the Royal Military Court," pages 676–80; Radek, "The SPD: Unity or Split?," pages 687–700.

Relations with Trotsky and 'Nashe Slovo'

Previous readings have illustrated some of the political differences between Lenin and the Bolsheviks, on the one hand, and Trotsky and the *Nashe Slovo* current among Russian Social Democratic exiles, on the other. The readings below focus on the Bolsheviks' efforts to draw these Russian revolutionists into joint political work around a revolutionary political perspective, seeking to win them to a consistent internationalist position.

- Background material, pages 346–51.
- The Bolsheviks' Proposal for Joint Action to *Nashe Slovo*, replies by *Nashe Slovo* and Trotsky, and comments by Lenin, pages 353–71.
- Trotsky, "Letter to Roland-Holst on 'Vorbote'," pages 520–24.

• Trotsky, "All the Conclusions Must Be Drawn," pages 596–98.

• Trotsky, "The Social Democratic Duma Fraction," pages 598–601.

• Trotsky, "Groupings in Russian Social Democracy," and Lenin's December 1916 evaluation of the evolution during the war of Trotsky and *Nashe Slovo*, pages 601–7.

• Lenin, "Open Letter to B. Souvarine," *Collected Works*, volume 23, page 202 (last paragraph) to page 204.

• "Mezhrayontsi Appeal for Revolutionary Unity," pages 607–9.

Strategy in the Russian Revolution

The Zimmerwald Left's positions found their fullest development in practice in the revolutionary activity of the Bolshevik Party. This activity was based not only on the Bolsheviks' political continuity going back to the beginning of the century, but also on the positions taken by them since August 1914 on the imperialist war, the bankruptcy of the Second International, and the fight for a new revolutionary world movement.

Part 5: Debates in the Zimmerwald Left

The Zimmerwald Left was not a politically homogeneous current. The only consistent revolutionary proletarian line within it was advanced by Lenin and the Bolshevik Central Committee majority that supported his views. This section of the study guide will focus on two of the questions that were most central to the debate within the Zimmerwald Left, as Lenin sought to win these forces to a Marxist line of march.

National liberation and self-determination

Differences on this question existed within the Zimmerwald Left from its founding. These differences came up over the discussion of alternative drafts of the resolution to be submitted by the Zimmerwald Left to the September 1915 conference. (Read the bottom of page 435 and the top of page 436.)

Lenin's views on the significance of the emerging struggles for national liberation to the worldwide struggle for socialism were developed in several important articles written prior to the outbreak of World War I. Three of these are reprinted in *Lenin's Struggle for a Revolutionary International* and should be read:

- "The Awakening of Asia," pages 168–70.
- "Backward Europe and Advanced Asia," pages 170–71.
- "The Historical Destiny of the Doctrine of Karl Marx," pages 172–75.
- As part of this reading, it is recommended that branches also read and discuss "Iranian Socialists and Kautsky Discuss Imperialism," pages 109–14. At this time, Kautsky presented a Marxist view of the relationship between the class and national struggle in a country oppressed by imperialism, such as Iran.

The debate on self-determination involved revolutionists both inside and outside the Zimmerwald Left, as well as in the Bolshevik Party itself. The main views in opposition to those of Lenin and the Bolsheviks are summarized in the readings below:

- Radek, "Imperialism and National Oppression," pages 525–32.
- Luxemburg, "National Self-Determination" (from "The Junius Pamphlet"), pages 635–37.

• Pyatakov (Kievsky), Bosh, and Bukharin, "Theses on Self-Determination," pages 545–49.

Lenin answered these arguments in numerous articles. Comrades should review page 27 of *Socialism and War* (pages 316–17 in volume 21 of the *Collected Works*), and read the following articles by Lenin:

• "The Socialist Revolution and the Right of Nations to Self-Determination," pages 532–45.
• "Reply to P. Kievsky," pages 549–56.
• "The Junius Pamphlet," pages 650–56.

Supplementary reading:

• Trotsky, "Nation and Economy," pages 558–60, and Trotsky, excerpt from "Letter to Roland-Holst on 'Vorbote'," page 524 (In conclusion. . . .). In addition, the key writings from the debate on this question by Lenin and Luxemburg from the years just before the war are listed in footnote 13 on pages 845–46.

A clear practical test of the counterposed lines on the question of national liberation struggles and self-determination during the period covered by this study guide was the 1916 "Easter Uprising" in Ireland. Read the following three selections:

• Trotsky, "Lessons of the Events in Dublin," pages 560–64.
• Radek, "The Song is Played Out," pages 564–67.
• Lenin, "The Irish Rebellion of 1916," pages 567–73.

The disarmament debate

• Jugend-Internationale, "Disarmament!" pages 779–83.
• Hansen, Norwegian Socialists on Disarmament, pages 783–85.
• Lenin, "The 'Disarmament' Slogan," pages 785–97.

Supplementary reading:
- Luxemburg, "Peace Utopias," pages 126–32.

Part 6: The struggle for a revolutionary movement in Germany and Russia

As the introduction to *Lenin's Struggle for a Revolutionary International* explains,

> Lenin waged a political struggle to influence and win the revolutionary Spartacist group in Germany led by Rosa Luxemburg and Karl Liebknecht. The Bolsheviks also made persistent proposals for collaboration to the Russian revolutionists around the left-centrist paper *Nashe Slovo* edited by Leon Trotsky. These forces were not part of the Zimmerwald Left during the period covered in this volume. The majority of them, however, responded to the revolutionary events in Russia in 1917, by, for the first time, charting a course that turned toward the revolutionary perspectives that Lenin and the Bolsheviks had been fighting for throughout the imperialist war, and rallied to the Comintern in 1919. (page 22)

Among the key differences separating the Bolsheviks from reformist, centrist, and other revolutionary forces in Russia was their political strategy for the Russian revolution. Comrades should review *Socialism and War*, pages 28–31 and 43–51 (pages 317–20 and pages 331–38 in volume 21 of the *Collected Works*).

The following are several important documents by the

Bolshevik leaders outlining their strategy for the Russian Revolution. Two of these articles—one by Lenin and one by Zinoviev—contrast the Bolsheviks' positions to those being advocated in *Nashe Slovo* by Trotsky. One of Trotsky's major *Nashe Slovo* articles on these questions is included in the readings.

- Lenin, "The Defeat of Russia and the Revolutionary Crisis," pages 414–19.
- Trotsky, "The Social Forces in the Russian Revolution," pages 575–84.
- Zinoviev, "War and the Revolutionary Crisis," pages 584–86.
- Lenin, "On the Two Lines in the Revolution," pages 586–90.
- Lenin, "Several Theses," pages 591–96.

Toward the new international

The deepening class polarization reflected inside the Zimmerwald movement and the rightward evolution of its centrist majority urgently posed the need—following its second conference held in Kienthal, Switzerland, in April 1916—to organize a new International. (Branches wanting to review the outcome of that conference can read pages 751–79, although this can be considered optional.)

- Lenin, "Imperialism and the Split in Socialism," pages 736–48.
- Kautsky, "For a Peace of Reconciliation," pages 803–06.
- Zimmerwald Left, "Social Democracy and the Question of Peace," pages 755–59.
- Lenin, "Theses for Appeal to the International Socialist Committee and All Socialist Parties," pages 810–22.

Supplementary reading:

- Zinoviev, "The Social Roots of Opportunism," pages 722–35.

Part 7: Summary discussion

Branches are encouraged to conclude this class series by rereading *Socialism and War* and conducting one or two class sessions on the pamphlet as a whole, in order to review the main political themes of the series.

John Riddell

Soviet Power and the Communist International

Lenin's writings on Soviet power and the Communist International (1918–1919)

THE OCTOBER 1917 REVOLUTION in Russia established the first revolutionary workers' and peasants' government.

This reading list is a guide to studying the Bolsheviks' perspectives during 1918 and 1919 on the character of such a government. It examines the course charted under V.I. Lenin's leadership toward launching a new, Communist International (Comintern) based on the victory in Russia and the impulse this gave to revolutionary struggles elsewhere.

The selections in this guide were written, with a few exceptions, in the years 1918–19—a time of major revolutionary struggles in parts of Europe and Asia. This period saw a broad debate in the world workers' movement on the lessons of the October revolution and on the Bolsheviks' call to build revolutionary proletarian parties and a new, Communist International.

This reading list is a companion to *Study Guide to Lenin's Struggle for a Revolutionary International* and other guides to the study of the writings of Lenin. Two books in the Pathfinder series The Communist International in Lenin's Time form the basis for the present outline. The first of these books, *The German Revolution and the Debate on Soviet Power,* deals with the months from October 1918 to February 1919, which led up to the launching of the Comintern. The second, *Founding the Communist International,* presents the proceedings of its first congress.

The heart of this study guide is Lenin's *The Proletarian Revolution and the Renegade Kautsky,* the entire text of which is included in these readings.

Three selections have been included from outside these two books on the Communist International. One of these is taken from the second volume of Farrell Dobbs's *Revolutionary Continuity.* The other two, which are found in Lenin's *Collected Works,* have been appended.

The study guide is designed for classes held in a seminar format, that is, classes consisting mainly of discussion by participants based on passages they have read and studied in advance. It may be appropriate to open the classes with presentations of five to ten minutes to fill in some background on particular events, individuals, or other matters dealt with in the reading.

Readings have been grouped here into sections covering different topics. Many of these will require more than one discussion session. Those using this guide to plan a class series should decide how long to spend on each topic, how to break down the weekly readings on that basis, and the nature of any opening presentations.

The length of readings selected for a class will vary depending on the character of the material. Some shorter sections of the guide—for example Lenin's "Draft Theses on the Agrarian Question"—deserve several study sessions. Other sections, which contain readings with more pages, can nonetheless be adequately covered in a seminar or two.

Some participants in this class series will already have read one or both of these books. Reading through them from beginning to end provides a graphic feel for the German revolution and the Comintern's founding congress of March 1919.

This guide approaches the books in a different way and for a specific purpose, that of enabling politically active revolutionary workers and students to study them collectively. It focuses on the two themes captured by the titles of these volumes: the debate on Soviet power and the founding of the new International, concentrating on the key writings of Lenin on these themes. In order to show the context within which these documents were written, a limited number of writings by the German revolutionists and by their class-collaborationist opponents within the workers' movement, such as Karl Kautsky, have also been included.

Substantial aspects of the two Comintern books have not been dealt with. In many cases only limited passages on a topic have been included in the study guide. Participants may find it profitable, as their time allows, to read the entire chapters on that topic.

When articles selected in this guide are preceded by commentary, these introductory passages are included in the assigned readings. They are included in the page numbers given below.

Most of the key writings in this study outline are also available in French and Spanish. In addition to Lenin's works, the first world congress proceedings and many writings of Rosa Luxemburg and Kautsky from this period can be found in French and Spanish translation. A partial list of these editions is given in the appendix.

The abbreviation *GR* has been used for *The German Revolution and the Debate on Soviet Power,* while *FCI* signifies *Founding the Communist International.*

Part 1: The German revolution and the Comintern's formation

Following the outbreak of revolution in Germany and elsewhere in central Europe in October and November 1918, workers faced the alternative of fighting to establish a revolutionary government of the workers and farmers or, failing that, being subject to the restoration of bourgeois rule. The challenge of launching such a struggle for power shook the workers' movement throughout Europe and North America. Communist currents, seeking to emulate the Bolsheviks' example, were formed in all the major countries of Europe.

Lenin's January 1919 article, "Letter to the Workers of Europe and America," which serves as a prologue to *The German Revolution,* explains the significance of these events and how they highlighted both the need for a new, Communist International and the prospects for its development.

- "Preface," in *GR,* pages 11–25.
- Lenin, "Letter to the Workers of Europe and America," in *GR,* pages 27–32.

Supplementary reading:

- "Introduction," in *GR,* pages 35–51.
- "The November Revolution in Germany," in *GR,* pages 70–104.
- "Organize the Power Anew from Below," in *GR,* pages 99–101.

Part 2: Power to the exploited or restored bourgeois rule

In the first days of November 1918, workers and soldiers in Germany rose in revolt, ousting the German emperor and organizing revolutionary councils to coordinate their struggle. The procapitalist leaders of the Social Democratic Party of Germany (SPD) sought to get the masses off the streets and to rein in the councils; the revolutionaries of the Spartacus League called for all power to go to the revolutionary councils.

Seeking to reestablish the authority of the institutions of the German capitalist state, leaders of the SPD such as Friedrich Ebert and Philipp Scheidemann, called for a national assembly to inaugurate a parliamentary system of rule. Karl Kautsky, while not a member of Ebert and Scheidemann's wing of the German Social Democracy, provided theoretical justifications for the SPD leadership's stand, arguing that a bourgeois parliament was more democratic than a government based on revolutionary councils of working people. Luxemburg, a central leader of the Spartacus League, explained its call for all power to the workers' and soldiers' councils.

- Friedrich Stampfer, "The Reich Government and the Workers' and Soldiers' Councils," in *GR,* pages 118–23.
- Luxemburg, "The Beginning," in *GR,* pages 123–27.
- Luxemburg, "The National Assembly," in *GR,* pages 139–44.

Bourgeois and proletarian democracy

The basis for Kautsky's defense of bourgeois rule in Germany had been laid earlier in 1918 by his attack on the Russian Soviet republic, entitled *The Dictatorship of the Proletariat.* Portions of the pamphlet are included in subsequent sections of this guide; Lenin also quotes from it extensively in his reply, *The Proletarian Revolution and the Renegade Kautsky.*

This section of the study guide contains the first two chapters of Lenin's reply, along with an attack by Kautsky on the Spartacus League that presents his basic position in summary form.

- Kautsky, "National Assembly and Council Assembly," in *GR,* pages 144–60.
- Lenin, "Preface" and "How Kautsky Turned Marx into a Common Liberal," in *GR,* pages 427–47.
- Lenin, "Bourgeois and Proletarian Democracy," in *GR,* pages 447–56.
- Lenin, "Can There Be Equality between the Exploited and the Exploiter?" in *GR,* pages 456–64.

Should revolutionary councils strive for state power?

Kautsky asserted that the soviets in Russia could play a progressive role only if they remained no more than a supplement to the trade union officialdom and parliamentary institutions and did not strive for state power. Lenin ridiculed this suggestion as a call to workers to "fight, but *don't dare win!*"

- Lenin, "The Soviets Dare Not Become State Organisations," in *GR,* pages 464–72.

The Russian Constituent Assembly

According to Kautsky and other opponents of workers' and peasants' rule, the Soviet government in Russia demonstrated its illegitimacy when it dispersed the Constituent Assembly in January 1918. The readings in this section take up, first, what this assembly was and how the Bolsheviks reacted to it and, second, Kautsky's comments on its dispersal and Lenin's reply.

• Lenin, "Theses on the Constituent Assembly," in *GR,* pages 403–10.

• Lenin, "Declaration of Rights of the Working and Exploited People," in *GR,* pages 410–13.

• Lenin, "Draft Decree on the Dissolution of the Constituent Assembly," in *GR,* pages 414–16.

• Kautsky, "Constituent Assembly and Soviets," in *GR,* pages 417–21.

• Lenin, "The Constituent Assembly and the Soviet Republic," in *GR,* pages 472–82.

The Soviet constitution

Kautsky's attack on the Soviet constitution focused on its political disenfranchisement of the exploiters. Lenin contended that this measure was not a necessary feature of the dictatorship of the proletariat but had "emerged of itself in the course of the struggle." Workers abroad would see this development, he said, as proof that "the Soviets are really organisations of the oppressed and not of social-imperialists and social-pacifists who have sold themselves to the bourgeoisie." The provisions of the Soviet constitution on this point are described in *FCI,* pages 456–57, note 26.

• Lenin, "The Soviet Constitution" (except for the final section), in *GR,* pages 482–91.

Record of the Soviet government

A central argument in Kautsky's case against the Bolsheviks, to which he repeatedly returned, was that their actions were founded on false hopes that Soviet-type governments would come to power across Europe. In reply, Lenin explained that proletarian internationalism could find expression only in a program directed toward the advance of revolution in Europe, Asia, and around the world.

• Kautsky, "The New Theory," in *GR,* pages 421–46.

• Lenin, "The Soviet Constitution" (final section only) and "What Is Internationalism?" in *GR,* pages 491–508.

Part 3: The worker-peasant alliance

The peasant question in the German revolution

Before proceeding to Lenin's views on the worker-peasant alliance, it is useful to study how this question was posed in the German revolution. There, the Communists had not yet fully broken from the pre-war German Social Democracy's sectarian position on the worker-peasant alliance.

• "Imperial Germany: The Road to Revolution," in *GR,* pages 38–40.

• "Toward a Worker-Peasant Alliance" (introductory notes), in *GR,* pages 293–307.

• Paul Frölich, "The German Peasantry and the Revolution," in *GR,* pages 311–12.

• Luxemburg, "Take the Class Struggle to the Countryside," in *GR,* pages 318–21.

• "Congress Debate on the Peasantry" and subsequent commentary in *GR,* pages 321–28.

The peasant question in the Russian revolution

Consistent with his stand in Germany, Kautsky opposed the revolutionary land reform carried out in Russia under

Soviet leadership. Lenin's response turned first to the role of the worker-peasant alliance in the successive stages of the October revolution. The second part of his reply (pages 521–34) defended the Soviet "Decree on Land" of November 1917 that nationalized the land and set the framework for its distribution.

Luxemburg supported the Soviet regime and recognized that the land reform "was an excellent tactic" to "bind the peasants to the revolutionary government." Yet in a draft manuscript written in prison in 1918 and not published at that time, she warned that division of the great estates among small peasants was a backward step that would block progress to socialism. The passage of her manuscript on this topic is included in this section.

- Luxemburg, "The Bolshevik Land Policy," in *GR,* pages 313–18.
- Lenin, "Subservience to the Bourgeoisie in the Guise of 'Economic Analysis,'" in *GR,* pages 508–38.
- Lenin, "Decree on Land," in *CW,* volume 26, pages 257–61.

The Communist International on the worker-peasant alliance

As we will see later in this class series, the founding congress of the Communist International in March 1919 was a relatively brief gathering with a limited agenda. Its main achievements were launching the new International and setting out the most fundamental axes of its program.

The agrarian question was touched on in *FCI* in the "Platform" (page 342) and in Lenin's report (pages 231–32). But it was not until a year later, at the second congress of the Communist International, that the lessons of the Russian revolution for building a worker-peasant alliance were debated and codified. These lessons were most clearly stated in Lenin's draft of the theses presented to the congress.

• Lenin, "Preliminary Draft Theses on the Agrarian Question," in *CW,* Volume 31, pages 152–64.

Part 4: The German Communist Party

The revolution that broke out in Germany in November 1918, the subsequent formation of the German Communist Party, and the murderous assault launched against it in January 1919 by the German Social Democratic leadership gave decisive confirmation to the lessons drawn by the Bolsheviks from the Russian revolution.

The story of the founding of the German Communist Party and of its debates and early struggles is told in *The German Revolution and the Debate on Soviet Power.* This section of the study guide includes three readings: Lenin's brief assessment of this experience, his summary comment on the historical role of Luxemburg, and a description of the German Communist Party's origin by Farrell Dobbs, taken from the second volume of his work, *Revolutionary Continuity.*

• Dobbs, *Revolutionary Continuity: Birth of the Communist Movement,* pages 40–44 and 66–77.

• Lenin, "A Letter to German Communists," in *GR,* pages 393–95.

• Lenin, assessment of Rosa Luxemburg, in *GR,* pages 395–96.

Part 5: Formation of the Communist International

'The Third International and its place in history'

In this article, written a few weeks after the Communist International's formation, Lenin discussed how a revolutionary government of the workers and peasants had come to be established in Russia in 1917 and how this fact gave the Comintern a different character from its predecessors.

- Lenin, "The Third International and Its Place in History," in *FCI,* pages 51–60.

Organizing the international communist congress

Since the collapse of the Second International in August 1914, the Bolsheviks had advocated formation of a new, revolutionary International. But it was the Russian revolution of October 1917 that laid the basis for creating this new organization. The process of forming the nuclei of revolutionary workers' parties in other countries received a big impulse. Not until the outbreak of revolution in Germany, however, did the Bolsheviks act to found such a new world organization.

According to Lenin, the foundation of the Communist International "became *a fact* when the German Spartacus League . . . made a clean break with . . . social-chauvinists (socialists in words, but chauvinists in deeds)" and "when the Spartacus League changed its name to the Communist Party of Germany" in December 1918. This action, along with the formation of Communist parties in several other European countries outside Soviet territory, convinced the Bolshevik leadership in December 1918 that the time had come to found the new, revolutionary International.

Lenin sketched the basis for a founding congress that month in a memorandum to G.V. Chicherin, the foreign minister of the Soviet republic. In January 1919, the call for the founding congress, drafted by Leon Trotsky, was published, and copies were sent across Europe by courier.

Before reading these documents, students may find it helpful to review the readings on the background to the founding congress given in part 1 of this guide. See *GR*, pages 27–32 and 40–51.

- Lenin, "To G.V. Chicherin," in *GR*, pages 587–90.
- "Letter of Invitation to the First Congress of the Communist International," in *GR*, pages 593–600.

The debate on founding the International

A significant obstacle to launching the new organization was posed by the opposition of the German Communist Party, the most authoritative revolutionary leadership outside the Soviet republic. The German party's view was nowhere recorded in writing, but the need to move decisively to constitute a new International was entirely absent from the party's founding congress in late December 1918 and from Luxemburg's writings at that time.

Because of the German party's resistance, when the March 1919 congress convened the Bolshevik leaders initially agreed to postpone launching the new organization. Nonetheless, the arrival of additional delegates and the impact of reports from abroad convinced the Bolsheviks and others to propose reopening the question.

- Eberlein, "A Conversation with Rosa Luxemburg on the New International," in *GR*, pages 603–5.
- "Introduction," passage dealing with congress preparations, in *FCI*, pages 25–26.

• "The Congress Opens," remarks by Lenin, Platten, Zinoviev, in *FCI,* pages 71–75.

• "The Decision to Found the International," remarks by Platten, Albert (Eberlein), and Zinoviev, in *FCI,* pages 237–43; vote and statement by Albert, pages 255–57.

• Lenin, "Won and Recorded," in *FCI,* pages 415–18.

Supplementary reading:

• Karl Steinhardt, "Report on German Austria," in *FCI,* pages 191–99, including note 16, pages 478–79.

• "Appendix: The Bolsheviks Evaluate the Congress," pages 418–35.

Part 6: The new international's program

The central programmatic document of the founding congress and of this study guide is the theses drafted by Lenin comparing the revolutionary rule of workers and peasants with bourgeois parliamentary regimes. This concluding section of the guide contains these theses, along with Lenin's report and resolution, which sought to give direction to the newly created Communist parties intervening in the revolutionary crises that had erupted in many parts of Europe.

• Theses, Report, and Resolution on "Bourgeois Democracy and the Dictatorship of the Proletariat," in *FCI,* pages 213–33.

Supplementary reading:

• "Platform of the Communist International," in *FCI,* pages 335–45.

- "Manifesto of the Communist International," in *FCI,* pages 310–24.
- "Resolution on the Need to Draw Women Workers into the Struggle for Socialism," in *FCI,* pages 347–48.

John Riddell

APPENDIX

French and Spanish editions of writings in this guide

French:

The writings of Lenin can be read in the French edition of his collected works.

Luxemburg's manuscript on the Russian revolution, her programmatic report to the Communist Party convention, and her article "Order Reigns in Berlin" can be found in *Oeuvres II,* printed by Maspero in 1969. The German Communists' program and Luxemburg's letter to Zetkin of January 11, 1919, were printed by Éditions sociales in 1969 in Luxemburg, *Textes.*

A French version of Kautsky's *The Dictatorship of the Proletariat* is included in a collection of Lenin's writings edited by Patrick Kessell and published in Paris in 1972 by the Union générale des éditions under the title, *La Révolution prolétarienne et le renégat Kautsky.*

For the first world congress proceedings, see Pierre Broué's edition, *Premier congrès de l'Internationale communiste,* published by EDI in Paris, 1974.

Spanish:

The writings of Lenin can be found in the Spanish edition of his collected works.

Luxemburg's manuscript on the Russian revolution and her programmatic report to the Communist Party convention are found in *Obras escogidas II* published by Editorial Pluma in Bogotá in 1976.

Editions of Kautsky's *Dictatorship of the Proletariat* and of the first world congress proceedings were published by Editorial Grijalbo in Mexico in 1975.

Wars:
Defensive and Aggressive

Wars: Defensive and Aggressive

BY GREGORY ZINOVIEV

The following article was written by Gregory Zinoviev in Switzerland in 1916–17 as a chapter of his book *The War and the Crisis of Socialism*. Zinoviev and Lenin were the two members of the Bolshevik Party Central Committee in exile during this period, and were jointly responsible for editing the Central Committee organ Sotsial-Demokrat and its other publications in exile. Zinoviev's book was a product of that collaboration.

Zinoviev's essay reprinted here replies to the social-chauvinists, who rallied to defend their ruling classes against rival imperialist powers in the First World War. These traitors to the working class rationalized their stand by referring to the positions of Marx and Engels on war in the earlier period of struggle for German unification and national liberation. Zinoviev's examination of the Marxist response to each of the major European wars and war crises from 1859 to 1911 helps fill out the historical background to the documents in *Lenin's Struggle for a Revolutionary International*. It is reproduced from the March, April, and May, 1939, issues of *New International*, theoretical magazine of the Socialist Workers Party.

IN THE COURSE OF the present war it has become a popular custom of the ruling class to portray the war as if "we" were the defensive side and the enemy the aggressor. This method has gained currency in Germany as well as in all the belligerent countries. And this happens for the purpose of exploiting the democratic traditions of the past epoch in the interest of present-day imperialist policy.

The defensive war once and now

The ideologists and agents of the bourgeoisie know that the division of wars into wars of defense and of aggression in the period of the national movements (about from 1789 to 1871) played a great rôle for the democratically-inclined elements.

They calculate quite rightly that the broad mass of the population can be duped most easily if they base themselves on the democratic ideology of times gone by. They know that during the epoch of 1789–1871 the division of wars of defense and of aggression found roots in the democratic masses that defensive wars were deemed to be in the order of things and just in those days, whereas wars of aggression evoked the indignation of the masses and their readiness to fight on the side of the defenders.

Only one little detail is necessary for the aim of the bourgeois imperialists to be attained: to carry over the criterion of defensive and aggressive wars to the new epoch, even though this division has now lost all meaning.

The bourgeoisie believes so much in this means that it seizes upon it in all states, without regard for the differences in form of government, language, culture, *etc.* The "technique" of which the German imperialist Ruedorffer spoke has acquired very wide dissemination. The German monarchy, parliamentary England, semi-absolutist Austria, Turkey and Bulgaria—all seize upon the "time-tested means." All of them, without exception, are allegedly conducting a war of defense.

All are defending themselves! Who then is the aggressor?

We have already said that the criterion of the defensive and aggressive wars has undergone the same change, with the passage of time, as the slogan of "the defense of the fatherland." The slogan of the "defense of the fatherland," like the criterion of the "just" war of defense, arose in the epoch of the *national* wars. At that time the defense of the fatherland meant at the same time the defense of national unity against foreign oppressors, it meant the struggle for the possibilities of developing a superior social order: *capitalism*, which was to replace feudalism.

This defense of the fatherland signifies *today*, in the imperialistic epoch, the support of finance capital, which claims as its own the army and the rest of the bourgeois state apparatus and seeks to prevent by violence the transition from capitalism to the meanwhile matured higher stage of development, *socialism*.

In the epoch of 1789–1871, the criterion of offensive and defensive wars helped to clarify for the masses where friend stood and where foe, where the oppressor and persecutor and where the defender of social progress. And what does this criterion mean today, in the year 1914? It helps the enemies of social progress deceive the popular masses, to mislead them as to where their common foe stands and where the only possibility of emancipating the peoples lies.

One may be sure that at any European congress of the Powers, the imperialist governments—despite all the antagonisms that separate them—would be unanimously of the view that the criterion of aggressive and defensive wars must absolutely be maintained. And they would be right from their standpoint. Let but all the peoples acknowledge this principle in itself; after that, it should not be very difficult to convince "our own" people that "we" are defending ourselves, while "they" are the aggressors.

The concept of wars of defense and of aggression

We have already pointed out that it is necessary to distinguish not only between two epochs, but also between two concepts: the defensive or aggressive war in the *historical* sense, and the defensive or aggressive war in the *diplomatic* sense. Let us elucidate this difference in greater detail.

What was understood by defensive and aggressive war in the epoch of national wars? How did the best representatives of democracy apply this criterion? What features were characteristic in determining which of the two species was involved? Did it suffice for country *X* to declare war upon country *Y* for country *X* to be considered the aggressor's camp and country *Y* the defender's?

Or: if in the war between *X* and *Y*, regardless of who first declared war, the armies of the former applied the strategy of the offensive and the armies of the latter the strategy of the defensive, did *that* suffice to consider the country *X* as the aggressor and the country *Y* as the defender?

Or: if both phenomena occurred at the same time, that is, if country *X* was the first to declare war and in addition her army invaded the land of the adversary, did *that* suffice to characterize country *X* as the aggressor?

No! Neither the diplomatic nor the strategical side exhaust the question. Another, much more important factor is decisive: the judgment from the standpoint of the *whole historical development*. Which of the two camps fought for the establishment of a national state, for the elimination of foreign rule and national dismemberment? Which of the two camps put an end, by this war, to the national movements within the country, in which country was the war preceded by years of national oppression and—as a reaction to it—long years of national struggles?

In other words: which of the two camps fought for historical progress? Only in this way could the question be decided. It was not just that state which first declared the war that was conducting a war of aggression; that might be the case, but again it might not be.

That state conducted a war of aggression which, by virtue of the whole situation, of the circumstances of the origin of the war, had to be acknowledged as the one that stood like an obstacle in the way of establishing an independent national-capitalist state.

That state conducted a war of aggression which, by means of the war, supported a policy that hampered historical progress in the above-described sense. And contrariwise: that state conducted no defensive war which first received the declaration of war which was first assailed by the adversary—that might be the case, but again it might not be.

That state conducted a defensive war which *defended* historical progress from the attacks of a powerful adversary; which conducted the war for the elimination of semi-feudal atomization, for the establishment of a national-capitalist state.

Capitalism represented, in comparison with feudalism, historical progress. In comparison with capitalism, only socialism can be recognized as historical progress. Hence, in the epoch of the national wars, a defensive war could be conducted only when the united national-capitalist state was defended against a feudal or semi-feudal atomization. Today, in the epoch of imperialist wars, when capitalism has reached the stage of its highest unfolding, a war of defense is possible only when a victorious *socialist* state is being defended against capitalist-imperialist states.

It is in this sense that Fr. Engels wrote in 1882 to Karl Kautsky that he does not rule out defensive wars after the victory of the proletariat, after its conquest of power; those would be wars in which the proletariat would be compelled to protect its socialist achievements against the capitalist states.[1]

---

1. *Kautsky, Sozialismus und Kolonialpolitik* (Socialism and colonial policy), 1907. At the beginning of the epoch of German imperialism, Kautsky turned to Engels with the question of how the English workers stood towards English colonial policy. Engels answered this in a letter of September 12, 1882. As this letter is of great interest, we should like to quote it here at length:

> You ask me what the English workers think of colonial policy. Well, exactly what they think of any policy—the same as what the middle classes think. There is, after all, no labour party here, only conservatives and liberal radicals, and the workers cheerfully go snacks in England's monopoly of the world market and colonies.
>
> As I see it, the actual colonies, i.e. the countries occupied by European settlers, such as Canada, the Cape, Australia, will all become independent; on the other hand, countries that are merely ruled and are inhabited by natives, such as India, Algeria, and the Dutch, Portuguese and Spanish possessions, will have to be temporarily taken over by the proletariat and guided as rapidly as possible towards independence.
>
> How this process will develop is difficult to say. India may, indeed very probably will, start a revolution and, since a proletariat that is effecting its own emancipation cannot wage a colonial war, it would have to be given its head, which would obviously entail a great deal of destruction, but after all that sort of thing is inseparable from any revolution.

Thus we must know how to distinguish between a war of aggression or defense in the *historical* sense—which is the essential—and a war of aggression or defense in the *diplomatic* (and strategical) sense—which is of secondary importance. There are cases in which a defensive war in the *historical* sense is a war of aggression in the *diplomatic*

> The same thing could also happen elsewhere, say in Algeria or Egypt, and would certainly suit *us* best. We shall have enough on our hands at home. Once Europe has been reorganized, and North America, the resulting power will be so colossal and the example set will be such that the semi-civilised countries will follow suit quite of their own accord; their economic needs alone will see to that.
>
> What social and political phases those countries will then have to traverse before they likewise acquire a socialist organisation is something about which I do not believe we can profitably speculate at present. Only one thing is certain, namely that a victorious proletariat cannot forcibly confer any boon whatever on another country without undermining its own victory in the process. Which does not, of course, in any way preclude defensive wars of various kinds.
>
> This business in Egypt [an upsurge against British and French colonial rule] has been contrived by Russian diplomacy. Gladstone is to take Egypt (which he is far from having or from holding, even if he had it), so that Russia may take Armenia; which would, according to Gladstone, be the liberation of another Christian country from the Mohammedan yoke. Everything else to do with the affair is pretence, humbug, prevarication. Whether the little scheme will succeed will soon become apparent. (*Collected Works*, Karl Marx, Frederick Engels, vol. 46, pp. 322–23.)

The conclusion refers to the occupation of Egypt by the English after the uprising of the Egyptians. A letter by Engels thereon of August 9, 1882 was recently published, in which he warned against judging the Egyptian national movement merely from the sentimental side. From this the conclusion was drawn that Engels had felt special sympathy for the annexation of Egypt by the English. We see here how little this was the case.

or strategical sense; and contrariwise.

Thus, for example, the wars of the Great French Revolution, of which we spoke in the first chapter. Even though they were often offensive wars in the diplomatic-strategical sense, they can nevertheless be characterized as *wars of defense* in the historical respect. Their historical significance consisted in this, that they had to defend the conquests of the Great French Revolution against the monarchies of the neighboring countries which endeavored to restore the old régime in France. If revolutionary France had not succeeded in offering resistance to the assault of England, which was already at that time fighting for her colonial predominance, if France had not held out in the wars against counterrevolutionary Austria—she would never have been able to defend and protect the conquests of 1789.

In order to be still clearer, we wish to adduce a few more examples. For the sake of brevity, we wish to employ only two terms from here on: the defensive war in the *historical* sense and the defensive war in the *diplomatic* sense.

The Italian War of 1859 as an example of a defensive war in the historical but not in the diplomatic sense

The Italian War of 1859 is the classic example of a national war. It was a typical war of defense, in the *historical* sense of the word. From the strategic-diplomatic standpoint, on the contrary, things were not so simple. For some time in Italy the national movement against Austrian foreign rule had been growing. After the Crimean War, the situation took on such shape from the diplomatic standpoint that Austria found herself more or less isolated on the international arena. Cavour, the main political leader of Piedmont, had every reason to assume that the given moment was favorable for an Italian war against Austria. He began to arm for the war, strengthened his army, recruited volunteers, *etc.* At the same time he also prepared a war in the *diplomatic* sense. He sought an ally and found one in Napoleon III.

Upon Napoleon's invitation, Cavour rode to him at Plombieres for a secret conference, and there they concluded in complete secrecy, without even the knowledge of the governments of the participating countries, an offensive alliance against Austria. Napoleon wanted above all to assure himself in a diplomatic way of Russia's neutral attitude. At the same time, however, all the necessary steps were taken to strengthen the two armies. All the details were worked out. France set up an army of 200,000 men which Napoleon himself was to command. Piedmont provided an army of 100,000 men. The armies were to unite at a given spot and carry through a given strategy. In case of a partial victory, Napoleon III was to receive Savoy as compensation; in case of a great victory, Nice in addition.

Cavour was so imbued with the desire to plunge into the long-awaited struggle for Italian independence, that he was ready to declare war upon Austria, even though such a challenge would create an unpleasant impression and show the whole world that this war, in *diplomatic* respects, was a war of aggression on the part of Italy. But Napoleon III acted more coldbloodedly and prudently. With the aid of all sorts of diplomatic artifices he endeavored to have the declaration of war come from Austria.

These dilatory methods of Napoleon III often drove Cavour to desperation. He believed that Louis Napoleon was imperilling the whole affair by his negligence. There was a moment in which it seemed that a diplomatic situation had been created in which war became altogether impossible. In despair, Cavour wanted to put an end to himself. That was the moment when England, on Austria's request, made the proposal to arbitrate the disputed questions at a congress, but on the condition that Sardinia first disarm, for otherwise the congress could not meet in peace, Napoleon III acted as if he was in agreement. He demanded only—that Austria should also disarm. Austria could not agree, for she knew well enough that all the war preparations had been made in Piedmont and that war must break out sooner or later. Besides, the financial position of Austria was such that she must either start the war immediately, or find herself unable to do it at all.

The war budget had reached its peak. After the beginning of the war Austria might put through internal loans under compulsion and suspend a number of payments, and in this way be able to overcome a financial crisis. But by postponing the war, Austria would only be creating new financial difficulties for herself. Thus Austria was compelled to declare war upon Sardinia. She sent the famous ultimatum: disarm within three days. When Cavour received this ultimatum, he was happy, because it *signified the war.*

Cavour was so overjoyed by this ultimatum that he almost fell on the neck of the Austrian ambassador who transmitted the document to him. He cried with joy like a child when his friends congratulated him on the impending war.

Austria, then, was the *first* to declare war upon Italy in 1859 and it was Austrian regiments who *first* crossed the enemy frontier. But in *diplomatic* respects Austria was not the aggressor, for the status quo was highly desirable for Austria; she did not want the war and would gladly have averted it. In *diplomatic* respects the war was one of aggression on the part of Austria's adversary. But in the deeper, in the only correct *historical* sense, it was nevertheless a defensive war for Italy, in which Italian unity, which meant an historical advance, was created and the semi-feudal national and state atomization eliminated.

What was the significance of the *diplomatic* duel between Napoleon III and Austria? Why was each side so anxious to have the declaration of war come from the other? Naturally, only because the directors of foreign policy wanted to exploit for themselves the impression which the first step makes upon the masses of the population. Every camp is anxious to present the enemy as guilty of the war in the eyes of the people.

Chernychevsky, a contemporary of those events, described the impression of the Austrian ultimatum as follows:

> The impudent ultimatum set all the neutral Powers and the public opinion of all Europe against Austria. Prussia, Russia, England protested against such behavior in the sharpest terms. The periodicals of all Europe were indignant over the senseless insolence of Austria. *The French Imperator triumphed: the Austrian cabinet could not have done anything to please him more.* Napoleon's whole diplomatic tactic was summed up in depicting Austria to Europe as guilty of the war, and now Austria had fulfilled his wish, even exceeding his hopes. (Vol. V, *Politics*.)

Farsighted people like Chernychevsky immediately recognized that *diplomatically* Austria was not guilty of the war. Naturally, the protesting neutral Powers also knew this, but for the broad masses of the people, for the millions, for the "periodicals of all Europe" which shape public opinion, Austria was considered the aggressor even in diplomatic respects.

This is what we learn from the Italian War of 1859. We see here very complicated relationships. Napoleon III stood by the side of Italy—out of quite selfish "compensation interests." He was as little concerned with national freedom as with the snows of yesteryear. He needed Savoy and Nice, he had to strengthen his authority in order to consolidate his position inside of France. In the Italian War, he appeared as the defender of historical progress—against his will. Similarly, reactionary Russia, by its neutrality, facilitated the Italian struggle against Austrian oppression.

And in spite of that, the War of 1859 was, in *historical* respects, a just war of defense on the part of Italy, that is, a war in which Cavour and Garibaldi stood on the side of progress and fought for the cause of bourgeois national-state unification against the feudal national and state atomization.

In 1859 Austria—from the historical standpoint—was the aggressor side *not because* she was first to declare war, *not* because her armies were the first to cross the enemy's frontiers. Austria was the aggressor side *even though* the diplomatic offensive tactic of Cavour and his allies forced Austria to declare war first. Italy (Piedmont) was the *defending* side in 1859 not because she received the Austrian ultimatum but *in spite of* the fact that she had provoked this ultimatum.

The *historical* significance of the war is decisive. The diplomatic preparation of the war plays an entirely secondary rôle.

A still greater interest in this respect is offered by the Franco-Prussian War of 1870–1871, temporally closer to us and in its own way just as classic an example. Let us follow the diplomatic pre-history of this last of the great national wars in Europe! It is worth while dwelling on the details.

The Franco-Prussian War of 1870–1871 as an example of a defensive war from the historical standpoint and an aggressive war from the diplomatic standpoint

Marx and Engels predicted that the inevitable result of the Austro-Prussian War of 1866 would be a new war. Nevertheless, the War of 1870 came quite unexpectedly to all socialists—and not them alone.

At the beginning of July, 1870, *i.e.*, scarcely two weeks before the outbreak of the war, the French Chamber of Deputies decided to reduce the number of recruits from 100,000 to 90,000. War Minister Lebeuf declared that he was in complete agreement with this reduction in the number of soldiers, for he himself wanted to underscore the pacific aspirations of his ministry. The president of the Council of Ministers, Olivier, declared, upon the interpellation of Deputy Jules Faure, that peace had never been so assured as at that moment, the political horizon was perfectly clear, there was currently no question that might engender any complications. Yet, in those very days, peace was already hanging by a hair. Behind the scenes the final preparations were being made for the war. . . .

Was the War of 1870–1871, in diplomatic respects, a war of aggression on Prussia's part and a war of defense on the part of France, or the other way around? Did Bismarck want this war; produce it and prepare it, or was it forced upon him by Napoleon? This is a question which is greatly disputed down to the present day. A whole series especially of German historians[2] continue even today to deny the fact of the forging of the notorious Ems dispatch by Bismarck.

At all events, in the beginning of the war everybody was of the opinion that the French government was the aggressor, while Prussia was only being forced to defend herself. Bebel tells in his memoirs that Liebknecht and he already suspected at that time that Bismarck was in reality the immediate aggressor: he had been arming for the war for years, and then brought it about; only, he knew how to dress the thing up from the outside in such a way that it looked as if Prussia had been attacked and only forced to defend herself. Yet—says Bebel—they had no proofs at that time which would enable them to make a flat assertion.

If more examples from history were needed to show that the criterion of the aggressive and defensive wars in the narrow, *i.e.*, the diplomatic sense of the term, was useless to the social democracy in the past epoch, the history of the German-French War could serve as a classic example. In estimating the diplomatic causes of the war, there were all sorts of opinions even among people who were intimate fellow-thinkers in all other ideological-political respects. All the circumstances were such that at the mo-

2. See, e.g., the presentation of this affair in the *Enzyklopaedie der neusten Geschichte* (Encyclopedia of modern history), published by Wilhelm Herbst, or *Die Geschichte des deutschen Reiches* (History of the German Empire) by Wilhelm Maurenbrecher. The same point of view is also defended by Charles Seignobos, *Politische Geschichte des neuen Europa* (Political history of modern Europe). In this work, the German socialists are reproached for having dared to accuse Bismarck of forging the Ems dispatch.

ment when the events unfolded it was actually doubtful who had been the immediate aggressor.

What were the circumstances when the war broke out in 1870–1871? The basis for the declaration of war was offered by the quite accidentally arisen question of the occupation of the Spanish throne. The throne had been offered to the Hohenzollern Prince Leopold. At first he thrice refused it, then he accepted it. The Prussian King Wilhelm I was completely indifferent to the affair, even hostile at the outset. He wrote to Bismarck that at bottom he was opposed to the enterprise.

But in the circles of the French government there was a desire to make a *casus belli* out of this candidacy. A Hohenzollern prince on the Spanish throne is a humiliation for France, a threat to French interests—these were the slogans of the French war party.

The affair dragged out for a year. But then the decision neared. Leopold was ready to place himself upon the Spanish throne. A terrific chauvinist frenzy began. Napoleon ordered his Ambassador Benedetti to go to King Wilhelm, who was taking the cure at Ems, and to force from him the commitment that the Hohenzollern prince renounce the Spanish throne. Wilhelm declared that this was a private affair which did not concern him. Benedetti, however, insisted, began to threaten—and the Hohenzollern prince withdrew his candidacy. Accidentally meeting the ambassador, the king joyfully communicated the information to him. Wilhelm added that happily the spectre of a military collision between France and Prussia had now finally disappeared.

But Napoleon and his clique were not satisfied with this. They raised a new demand: Wilhelm must most solemnly *guarantee* that in the *future* also he will under no circumstances allow anyone from the House of Hohenzollern to accept the Spanish throne. If Prussia should not give the guarantee, France will know how to defend its interests and not recoil from the most resolute measures. This signified a direct threat of war. Nevertheless Wilhelm granted Ambassador Benedetti an audience again and explained to him very loyally that there was no need of a guarantee and that France could rest quite easy, now that Prince Leopold had renounced the Spanish throne. He permitted Benedetti to use his words in an official communication to the French government.

Benedetti established contact with his government and received the instruction to demand solemn guarantees *at all costs*. Once more he sought King Wilhelm. The king granted him no audience, but informed him through his adjutant that Leopold's renouncement of the Spanish throne was final, and that peace was in no way imperilled. All the rest the French ministry could handle with the Prussian cabinet in the usual way.

At the same time, Abeken, on Wilhelm's instruction, sent a detailed dispatch to Bismarck in which the events of the recent days, the negotiations with Benedetti, *etc.*, were communicated in a wholly peaceful tone. Bismarck was given the right to make this communication public in the press if he should deem it necessary.

When the dispatch arrived from Ems—Bismarck himself recounted later—he was at luncheon with Moltke and Roon. After he had scanned the dispatch, he handed it to his colleagues. When they had read the Ems dispatch, they lost their appetites: they saw that the affair was taking a peaceful turn and that all their hopes for an immediate war were destroyed. Thereupon Bismarck—as he himself recounts—took the telegram from their hands and sat down at a small side-table. Five minutes work—and the dispatch looked quite different. When Bismarck showed it to Moltke and Roon in its revised form, their spirits became cheerful again. "Now it sounds quite different," opined the taciturn Moltke. "Before it was a drumbeat, now it's a trumpet blast!" And the small but jolly company sat down again at the luncheon table with a new appetite.

Now it was clear that the war would have to come. The provocatively forged Ems dispatch was made public in the press of the entire world and there was a terrific ferment in Napoleon's circles. On July 19 France declared war on Prussia. The French Chamber of Deputies approved this important decision of the Napoleonic government against the opposition of a small minority.

That is what the external history of the origin of the Franco-Prussian War looked like. Who then was the aggressor from the diplomatic standpoint, and who the defender?

In his exceptionally interesting memoirs, Bismarck insists that France brought about the war. But from the facts which he himself describes it appears clearly and plainly that he, Bismarck, was the one who prepared and brought about the war.

Bismarck tells how on the night after the battle of Sedan he rode out with a group of superior officers to inspect the battlefield. It was very dark. Bismarck did not know all the officers who were in his suite. The talk ran to the causes which had directly brought about the war. Bismarck observed that he was absolutely unable to understand the French, for he had always believed that the candidacy of

Prince Leopold for the Spanish throne was agreeable, if anything, to the French. The personal relations of Prince Leopold to the French court had always been excellent. Besides, once on the Spanish throne, he would have had to pursue a *Spanish* and not a Prussian policy. But since Spain bordered France and shared many common interests with her, Spain would have to endeavor to live in peace with her powerful neighbor. Nobody would have been able to demand that Spain take the part of Prussia against France.

Quite unexpectedly for Bismarck, a voice of protest suddenly rang out from the darkness. Among the officers was Prince Leopold himself, and he protested against the assertion that he, the Hohenzollern prince, could have had any sympathies for France.

Bismarck perceived that Prince Leopold had to protest under the given circumstances and he even apologized to him. But from this incident, Bismarck contended, it was perfectly clear that he had no special desire to see Prince Leopold on the Spanish throne.

Perhaps that was indeed the case. The Spanish throne in itself could not hold any particular attraction for Bismarck. But the Spanish episode was very welcome to him as an irreplaceable cause of war. Primarily because it was a cause which offered the possibility of attributing the guilt to the opponent. Bismarck says in his memoirs that he was always of the opinion that victorious wars can be easily justified only when they are forced upon one (or, *appear* to the people to have been forced upon one, he might have said).

In any case, the incident which Bismarck narrates proves nothing of essential importance to the question. How greatly Bismarck desired the war is to be seen from the fact that—according to his own story—he wanted to retire when it appeared that the Spanish incident would be settled in a peaceful manner. He had already communicated his firm decision to War Minister Roon and to General Moltke. He could not brook such "international insolence" on the part of France! He could not sacrifice his honor and the honor of Prussia for the sake of "politics." A "retreat" by Prussia in the Spanish conflict would have meant a humiliation.

His resignation was decided upon. He already had it in his pocket. Suddenly a new ray of hope flashed. The Ems dispatch arrived. "Without adding a word" he only "reduced" it and so altered "the wording" that the "difference" in the effect of the abbreviated text . . . was not the result of the stronger words, but only of the form, which made the document appear peremptory, whereas in Abeken's edition it would have appeared only as a fragment of the suspended negotiations which were to be continued in Berlin. (*Gedanken und Erinnerungen von Otto Fürst von Bismarck* [Reflections and reminiscences of Otto, Prince von Bismarck], vol. II, chapter on the Ems dispatch.) Only! Nothing more and nothing less. . . .

The Spanish incident came as a boon to Bismarck also because he hoped (see his memoirs) that Spain would be indignant over the interference of France in her internal affairs and would likewise declare war on France. As is known, this did not happen. "Spain left us in the lurch," Bismarck observes melancholically.

Bebel tells in his memoirs that the thorough fighting preparedness of the Prussian army at the moment of the war's outbreak made a deep impression upon him and his friends. This fact opened the eyes of Bebel and his fellow-thinkers as to where the immediate aggressor was to be sought. On the other hand, however, it appeared clearly from many important episodes prior to the declaration of war that the government of Napoleon was calling forth the war. Of the falsifying of the Ems dispatch nobody at that time had the slightest notion. This "official secret" was carefully kept by German diplomacy. It does great honor to the perspicacity of Wilhelm Liebknecht that, as early as 1873, right after the appearance of the official communication of the Prussian General Staff on the Franco-Prussian War, he recognized that the Ems dispatch had been forged and that he attributed this falsification to Bismarck—openly in the press.[3] But at the beginning of the war not even Liebknecht saw all the finesse of Bismarck's game.

Three decades after these events, Jaurès wrote a whole treatise on the Franco-Prussian War. He was interested least of all, of course, in justifying Bismarck and Bismarckian Prussia. But from his arguments it is clear that a large share of the guilt for the war of 1870–1871 fell upon Bonapartist France. In any case, it is clear that the situation was very complicated and confusing, so that at the moment when the events were unfolding, it was very difficult to ascertain on which side the direct guilt for the war was to be sought.

Since 1867 Bismarck had been intriguing systematically to force France into a war. The Spanish incident was very convenient for him, for it created conditions that enabled him to make it look to the outside world as if France was the immediate aggressor. On the other hand, says Jaurès, Louis Napoleon made spasmodic efforts throughout 1869 to establish an offensive alliance of France-Austria-Italy

3. See the articles of Liebknecht in *Volkstaat* (People's state), reprinted in his pamphlet *Die Emser Depesche oder wie Kriege gemacht werden* (The Ems Dispatch, or how wars are manufactured), Nuremberg, 1891.

against Prussia. Austria displayed the greatest irresolution, for it feared to attack Prussia, but was absolutely inclined to conclude a defensive alliance against Prussia. Up to the very eve of the declaration of war in July 1870, Napoleon's diplomacy was firmly convinced that Austria would actively support France against Prussia.

Bismarck employed all sorts of ruses. Jaurès supposes that Bismarck, Roon and Moltke—while the conflict was developing—intentionally went to the health-resort in order to maintain their alibi before the wide public and to attribute to France with all the greater success the whole guilt for the coming of the war. The French minister de Gramon, in Jaurès' opinion, behaved like a man who had been thrown into complete confusion. He delivered threatening speeches, he sought to unleash the passions, he made impossible demands. Even after Leopold's renouncement of the Spanish throne, Benedetti telegraphed de Gramon that further demonstrations on the part of France would inevitably provoke a war. But the Bonapartist ministry continued the policy it had already adopted. It believed that the moment was favorable for an attack upon Prussia.

At the last moment, certain influential members of the Chamber of Deputies sought to stop the war. Thiers declared that it was madness (*"c'est une folie"*) on the part of the French government. Others joined in with him. But—it was too late. The conflict had gone too far.

Jaurès characterizes the situation as follows: *two* nets of intrigue had been spun beyond raveling for several years before the war. On the banks of the Seine the war had been just as ardently prepared as on the banks of the Spree. Bismarck proved to be the foxier. Now, after the events, this is clear. But the responsibility for the war falls also upon

Bonaparte's adventuristic government.[4]

Another French socialist (now we can say—former socialist), who also never had any particular sympathy for the Germans, Gustav Hervé, did not venture as late as 1905 to say with certainty which side had been the aggressor in 1870. "France was the first to declare war," writes Hervé, "but if it is true that Bismarck, as he himself asserts, falsified the notorious Ems dispatch, it must be acknowledged that the German government bears at least half the responsibility for the declaration of war." (Gustav Hervé, *Leur Patrie* (Their country), p. 135.)

The example of the Franco-Prussian war shows us one thing as plain as day: the formal criterion which is supposed to show who was the first to attack, who was the first to declare war, offers the social democracy *no* point of departure for establishing its tactic in connection with the war. Had the German social democrats applied only this formal criterion during the Franco-Prussian War, they would have made a multitude of mistakes and would scarcely have fulfilled their duty.

In the strategical-diplomatic respect, Napoleon III began this war. He was the first to declare war, his regiments were the first to cross the frontier. But on the other hand the facts have shown that Bismarck *forced* him into it by cunning maneuvres—just as Napoleon III forced Austria into such a step in 1859. At the moment of the event—when the highly complicated situation is considered—even the

---

4. See *Histoire Socialiste*, vols. VI, XI; *La guerre Franco-Allemande* (The Franco-Prussian War) by Jean Jaurès, pp. 163, 166, 169, 175–6, 178–9. 102, 241, in the chapter "*Qui est responsable de la guerre?*" (Who is responsible for the war?). See also the interesting article on Jaurès' book by van Ravenstejn in *Die Neue Zeit*, 1908, vol. I, pp. 388 ff.

most advanced men of those days could not correctly recognize the connection of things. From this arose many mistakes. But to appeal to these mistakes, to elevate them to a theory, as the social-chauvinists are now doing—means to muddle the question deliberately.

Formally, considered from the diplomatic standpoint, Napoleon III was guilty of the war. *Actually*, Bismarck was much guiltier. But the question of who was guilty in the diplomatic respect recedes into the background before the question of the *historical* significance of this war, which is what is important for the whole world. In the *historical* respect it was absolutely a question for Germany of a defensive war—and Bismarck's machinations cannot alter that in the slightest. Bismarck might have been the first to declare war, just as in 1859 Cavour was almost the first to begin the war.

Bismarck's intrigues might have been dirtier than they were in reality. In the *historical* respect Prussia would nevertheless have been conducting a defensive war. Why? Because for Prussia, as we have already emphasized so often, it was a question of the historically necessitated unification of Germany and of the elimination of feudal atomization. Because Bonapartist France had stood for a long time as a direct hindrance on the road to this unification, because Napoleon III sought absolutely to prevent it. His whole position in Europe was conditioned upon the national atomization of Germany.

Even as early as 1866 Napoleon III endeavored, as we saw, to acquire "compensations" on the German side of the Rhine. Napoleon III was now the *main enemy* who sought to prevent the German unification. A victory over Napoleon III had to result in two important facts. *First*, the unification of Germany: if successful, a unification from below, on the revolutionary path; if not, then unification from above, through Bismarck. *Second*, France would be liberated from Bonapartism; with Louis Napoleon, the worst representative of European reaction would be removed.

For this reason—quite independently of who was the instigator of the war from the *diplomatic* standpoint—it is correct to say that in the *historical* respect Napoleon was the aggressor and Germany the defender. From this perfectly correct view, many socialists of that time drew the entirely false conclusion that for this reason they must adopt the standpoint of Bismarck, vote for war credits, declare civil peace, become bourgeois patriots, *etc*. But this conclusion was completely false. Even in national wars the socialists have their specific tasks. Marx and Engels, Liebknecht and Bebel, as we saw in the preceding chapters, gave an example of *socialist* conduct even in such situations.

The war of 1877–1878 as a transition to a new era

We have already said that the war of 1870–1871 was the last great national war in Europe to which—proceeding from the interests of socialism and of democracy—the criterion of the aggressive and defensive wars, in the historical sense of these terms, could be applied.

And the war of 1877–1878? Was it not a national war too? This question may be answered with a Yes and a No.

For the Serbs, Bulgarians, Rumanians, *etc*., it was a question of national independence and the war, for them, bore a national-emancipatory character. The echo of the national struggle was heard in all the events of 1876, 1877 and 1878 on the Balkan peninsula; national uprisings followed military clashes.

On the other hand, however, all the events occurred under the sign of the imperialist race between Russia and England. These two Great Powers made the small Balkan peoples their tools, although it was a life and death question for the latter. This was most clearly discernible from the Berlin Congress. Imperialist England, basing herself on her sea power and exploiting the antagonism between Russia and Austria, forced Russia into a revision of the San Stefano Treaty.

To the Berlin Congress in 1878—like a swarm of crows—rushed the diplomats of the European Powers, bent on chiselling the juiciest possible morsels for their governments. England obtained the Island of Cyprus, Russia took Bessarabia again and received Batum, Ardagan and Kars in addition. Austria obtained a protectorate over Bosnia and Herzegovina. Bismarck, as "honest broker," was promised various advantages for German trade in the Dardanelles and the Bosporus. Russia got most of all; the Sultan had to "cede" more than 30,000 square kilometers.

It became known later on that France was then secretly guaranteed Tunis by England. Thereupon, in 1881, France, with Bismarck's permission and England's tacit support, seized Tunis. Cyprus for Tunis, Tunis for Cyprus! The Bulgarians and Serbs were fighting for their national independence; that gave France cause enough for stealing Tunis in Africa! One of the best proofs that, as early as the war of 1877–1878, imperialist motives played an enormous role—at least among the principal stage-managers of the drama.

What has the struggle for genuine national independence to do with the imperialist raids which England and the other imperialist Great Powers undertook in this war?

The Bulgarian peasant of course put his heart and soul

into this war. He was really fighting for national emancipation. The unheard-of pressure exercised by the Turks had called forth a strong national movement. The economic and cultural subjugation was especially aggravated by the pressure exerted in religious affairs. When the Bulgarian soldiers heard the church-bells of the field churches built by Karl of Rumania, they went into ecstasy. These church-bells were like manna from heaven to them. The Turks had prohibited the Bulgarians for many years from having bells in the churches. To the Bulgarian peasants, the sound of the bells was a harbinger of emancipation from the Turkish yoke.

But the real directors of the affair—the imperialists of England, France, *etc.*—had an interest in a quite different sound, the sound of money, of gold which was to be squeezed out of the traded-off territories. National unity in itself interested them very little. The result of the war was that the Serbian people was suddenly split into four parts: the Serbian parts of Turkey and Austria, Montenegro and its own land. The Bulgarians were divided into two parts. So were the Rumanians. The bourgeoisie of the Great Powers, without the slightest compunction, completely split up the small peoples who had joined the struggle for their national independence.

The war of 1877–1878 showed that even in so remote a corner of Europe as the Balkan peninsula, the Great Powers immediately intervene, and the elements of the national struggle are finally completely lost in their imperialist world struggle. The criterion of defensive and aggressive wars was historically outdated. A new era dawned in which, according to the whole state of things, such a criterion had lost all meaning. The war of 1877–1878 constituted the transition to this new era. In subsequent wars, the national element played a certain role. But this role was an entirely subordinate one. We are ready to admit that even in the war of 1914–1916 there are remote corners of Europe where the national element still plays a small role—the national element in the Austro-Serbian conflict. But that is only an episode, a small detail which alters nothing in the imperialist character of the war.

The diplomatic-strategical estimation of the wars of defense and aggression could never serve democracy as a criterion. The examples of the Italian and the Franco-Prussian wars show that. So do the wars of the Twentieth Century. Examples: the Balkan war of 1912 (*i.e.*, the war of the Slavic peoples against Turkey) and the second Balkan war of 1913 (*i.e.*, the war of the Slavic peoples among themselves). If the criterion is applied from the diplomatic standpoint, entirely different results are attained. It was not the Turks who declared the war—the *status quo* was in their favor—but the Slavic peoples. Could democracy therefore take the part of Turkey, which was allegedly attacked? Of course not! In 1913, Bulgaria started the war, not Serbia. *Bulgaria* was—in diplomatic respects—the directly guilty party (we disregard here the role of Russia). Could democracy draw the conclusion from this that it must take the part of Serbia against Bulgaria?

With the beginning of the new era, the old yardstick has become obsolete also in *historical* respects. For the whole environment, all the conditions, have become different. Once Wilhelm Liebknecht maintained that in case of an aggressive war, democracy is under obligation to support those who are defending themselves; he compared the aggressive party with a simple thief and robber who breaks into someone else's house to carry off something which the proprietor of the house himself requires.

Now it is different. In the imperialist epoch wars are conducted by a whole series of consummate thieves and robbers *for the division of the wealth (and lives) of third persons.* There is nothing for honest people to do in this case but to find the shortest way of rendering harmless *all* these thieves, the whole gang. When two house-breakers are quarreling over the spoils—what honest man worries over which of the two was the first to violate the thieves' code of morals? It is positively ridiculous to speak here of the criterion of a just war of defense. . . .

Modern slaveholders

In a certain sense, *all* the wars of the non-European peoples, who have been turned into mere *objects* of imperialist policy, are "just" wars of defense. These peoples are divided arbitrarily. Dissections are performed on their living bodies. The European imperialists trade them off like cattle. The imperialist Great Powers of Europe divide whole continents among themselves.

When Wilhelm II, shortly before the outbreak of the Russo-Japanese war, sent Nicholas II the famous telegram: "The Admiral of the Atlantic Ocean salutes the Admiral of the Pacific Ocean"—what did this mean politically? It meant that the German imperialists were proposing to the Russian Czar and the Russian imperialists to suppress all the peoples of Asia on the condition that the Czar and the Russian capitalists do not prevent the German imperialists from suppressing and exploiting all the peoples of Africa. It was a proposal to divide the slaves among the slaveholders.

The population of the colonies means nothing but beasts

of burden to the gentlemen imperialists. A small example: In 1904 occurred the uprising of the Hereros in the Southwest African colony of Germany. The hapless native population could no longer stand the pain and torment to which they were subjected for years by the merchants of civilization sent by Wilhelm II. The German merchants plundered the population and reduced it to beggary. The German officers and gendarmes beat and killed the unfortunate Hereros—women and children were pitilessly mistreated—in the interest of maintaining "discipline." When the Hereros rebelled, Wilhelm sent down new regiments. *Half* the male population of the colony was killed. The Hereros and their families were driven by the thousands into the burning, waterless desert, where they died of thirst. . . .

Ten years have passed since these inhumanities; the Germans feel the shortage of working forces in that colony—and now they are sorry: How "inexpediently" we acted, they say, why did we so senselessly murder off so much toiling cattle? One of the most prominent representatives of German imperialism, Paul Rohrbach, writes in 1915 in his book, *Unsere koloniale Zukunftsarbeit* [Our future work in the colonies], the following cynical words:

> When the uprising [of the Hereros] broke out, its suppression was not left to the then Governor Leutwein and his experienced old officers. Instead a commander-in-chief was sent down who had no notion that—in the later word of Dernburg—the natives are the great economic asset of an African colony. A war of extermination was declared against the Hereros and something like half the people perished in the foodless and waterless

> desert. Likewise did all the cattle fall victim to the inexpedient [!] conduct of the war. Of course the rebels had to be punished and, above all, disarmed, but to exterminate half of them was as absurd as it could possibly be. The dangerous labor shortage now prevalent in Southwest Africa derives mainly from the conduct of the war of 1904–1905. It is responsible for the present slowing down of the economic development of the colony. (Paul Rohrbach, *Unsere koloniale Zukunftsarbeit*, Stuttgart, 1915, pp. 29f.)

Aren't these the words of a slaveholder?

The imperialists of *all* countries treat the peoples who are the objects of their imperialist exploitation as slaves. Naturally the slaves rebel against their tormentors and naturally the strivings of these peoples for freedom and independence become stronger the more often they have the opportunity to conduct a war of defense against their oppressors.

The socialists must recognize these wars of the colonial peoples against their European imperialist rulers as just wars of defense. And that quite independently of who is the immediately aggressive party.

The Boer War from the standpoint of aggression and defense

In 1877, the English imperialists declared the Boer Republic a part of England. For many years, they employed all sorts of violent measures until—basing themselves upon a petition of 2,500 (!) Boers who were supposed to have begged voluntarily for incorporation into England—the

English imperialists decided to act more energetically. At first the Boers submitted. In 1881, however, they assembled enough forces and, under the leadership of Kruger, Praetorius and Joubert, they attacked the English army which suffered a heavy defeat.

That was the first act of the Boer drama. The Boers began once more. On October 9, 1899, the government of the Boer Republic sent the English government an ultimatum consisting of four points: 1. the conflict must be decided by a court of arbitration; 2. England must withdraw her armies from the frontier; 3. all reserves sent to South Africa from June 1 onward, must be recalled to England; 4. the armed forces being sent on warships must not be landed anywhere in South Africa.

Without waiting for any of the formalities connected with the consideration of the ultimatum by the English House of Commons, the Boers attacked the English troops. They were the aggressive party and England, formally, the defender. And the English proclaimed to the entire world that their war was a just one, they had been assaulted, *etc.* In spite of this, the Boer war was a just war on the part of the Boers and the world proletariat took their part.

Why? Because the Boer people was fighting for its independence.[5] English imperialism, however, was fighting for the capture of the diamond fields discovered in Kimberley in 1867.

For decades the English imperialists had oppressed the Boers, exploiting them politically and economically. In 1896 the English representative in South Africa, Jameson, launched a cavalry attack upon the Boers, during which

5. This did not prevent the Boers from exploiting a part of the natives.

many innocent citizens lost their lives. He declared later that he was forced to act in "self-defense." In reality, however, the English rifles had gone off a little sooner than was suitable for the plans of the English government. It was compelled to act as if it was dissatisfied with its representative. He was turned over to a court, given thirteen months in prison, but was then pardoned because of "poor health." This was just as hypocritical a comedy on the part of the English imperialists as the famous telegram of sympathy which Wilhelm II sent the Boers on the occasion of the event. The English and the German imperialists played with the Boers like a cat with a mouse.

Hence the war of the Boers against the English was outwardly a war of aggression—in reality, a just war of defense.

The Abyssinian War considered from the same standpoint

Or a second example: Abyssinia's war against Italy in 1896.

Since 1881, Italy had been taking over one Red Sea territory after another. The gold, ivory, rubber, coffee, cotton and other fields increasingly whetted the appetite of the Italian imperialists. On May 2, 1889, Humbert, King of Italy, succeeded in tying down Menelik to a treaty which brought Abyssinia into complete economic dependence upon Italy. In 1894–1897, Kassala already also belonged to the Italians, who then sold it to the English for cash money.

The Italian imperialists felt themselves more and more "at home" in their Eritrean colonies. But in order to guarantee these colonies for good, the Italian Premier Crispi took care to strengthen constantly the Italian army stationed there. In 1896 he decided to increase it by 10,000 men. Thereupon Menelik, without waiting for the 10,000 new Italian soldiers, attacked the Italians with an army of 90,000 men and on March 1, 1896 inflicted a complete defeat upon them at Abba Kapima. In December the Italian-French-English treaty was signed, recognizing the independence of Abyssinia and establishing only the principle of the "open door."

Thus Abyssinia was the *first* to declare the war on Italy in 1896. Outwardly, therefore, Abyssinia was the aggressive party, but in reality she was conducting a just war of defense against the Italian imperialists.

China and the Great Powers

Let us consider China. This country has especially excited the appetites of the Great Powers. Let us dwell upon her in some detail.

As a classic example of the wars of suppression of the period which directly preceded the imperialist epoch, there is the war which England conducted against China in 1840–1842 over the buying of opium.

English trade in China was a monopoly of the English East India Company. In the interests of its enrichment, the company adapted itself fully to the orders of the Chinese authorities; the latter looked down upon the "barbarians" from the West and were of the opinion that the "barbarians" had the right of trade in China only thanks to the special grace of the Son of Heaven. The English capitalists resisted such a conception of their rights.

On April 22, 1834, the monopoly of the English East India Company was abolished by the English Parliament (Wilhelm Schuler, *Abriss der neueren Geschichte Chinas,* [An outline of modern Chinese history] Berlin, 1912, p. 128).

England made an effort to acquire the right of free trade in China.

As early as 1834–1836, matters almost reached the point of military conflict over the question. England attempted to settle down in China; she had the conception that according to the prevailing international law the non-Christian peoples in general were not all equal. That is how a defender of English policy, Eitel, explains England's conduct (*The History of Hongkong*).

In this already tense situation, the conflict over opium trade played a decisive rôle.

The opium trade reached an enormous scope in China. At the beginning of the Nineteenth Century, the number of annually imported opium cases reached 4,100, that is, twenty times as large as twenty years earlier. In 1820, 10,000 cases were imported, in 1830, 18,000 cases, in 1835, 30,000 (*Loc. cit.*, p. 134).

Against this trade in opium, which was most harmful to the Chinese population because it promoted dipsomania, sickness and degeneration, the Chinese government made emphatic protest. Smuggling was severely punished. The Chinese commissioner, Liu, confiscated and destroyed 20,283 cases in 1839. In spite of this, the Indian opium crop continued to be imported into China.

Liu proceeded to more incisive methods. He forced all Englishmen to withdraw to Hong-kong. And although Liu proposed quite acceptable conditions for the opium trade to the Englishmen in November 1839, England nevertheless decided to launch a war.

The war began. On January 26, 1841, the English occupied Hong-kong. The cruelty of the English knew no bounds. The Chinese offered desperate resistance to the "inferior beings against whom gods and men rebelled". The Chinese would not allow themselves to be captured alive by the English. In Chinese camps about to be occupied by the English, the Chinese, before surrendering to the superior forces of the English, killed their wives and children and then committed suicide. The Chinese regimental commanders—officers and generals—preferred to do away with themselves, to burn on a funeral pile, rather than fall into the hands of the English. So great was the cruelty of the English and so great the hatred of the Chinese.

England of course triumphed over unfortunate China. The peace was signed in Nanking on August 29, 1842. The Island of Hong-kong passed into the hands of the English in perpetuity on the basis of the peace treaty. Canton, Shanghai and other ports were made free for English trade. The system of monopoly was abolished. England gained the right to send her consuls to China. China paid $21,000,000 for the destroyed opium, for war indemnity, *etc.*

Therewith began the great European expeditions against China.

The peace of 1842 improved the tense relationships between England and China only for a short time. China was unable to offer resistance to the assault of the European Powers. The impending partition of China was openly discussed in the European press. Napoleon III joined hands with the English imperialists. In 1856–1860, China was forced into a war against England and France. The hatred of England mounted higher. A conspiracy was uncovered in Hong-kong which aimed at poisoning all the Englishmen resident there. The plan failed only because the food (sandwiches) contained too large a dose of arsenic. So great was the embitterment of the Chinese.

The English insisted upon an extension of their rights in China. They began a new war, bombarding and destroying whole cities. In 1858, they dictated to China the peace of Tientsin. England succeeded in having something like ten more Chinese ports opened up to English trade. The trade tariffs were altered in England's favor, the right to send an English ambassador to China was recognized, China paid indemnities, *etc*. One of the points of the peace treaty (7.) read: the term "barbarians" may no longer be applied to any English subject. (*Loc. cit.*, p. 172.)

Such are the methods by which the imperialists restored their "honor" and thus did they retort to the notion about their "barbarism".[6]

The second imperialist power acted in the same way. Atrocities which the Chinese committed against French officials were avenged by the French troops in such a way—just before the conclusion of the peace—that 200 castles and temples and a very valuable library were burned. Then they dictated a peace to the Chinese in Peking which was in harmony with that of Tientsin and in some points even worse.

In November 1860, General Ignatiev forced China not only to confirm the treaty of Aigun but in addition to cede the whole territory east of the Ussuri to Russia.

In 1880, Japan took possession of the Chinese island of Tsiukin.

---

6. The European Great Powers illustrated their antipathy to "barbarism" in 1901 when they concluded a "peace" with China following the Boxer uprising. After this peace treaty, a number of Boxer leaders were beheaded. In addition, the Chinese government was forced by the "Great Powers" to abandon the corpse of the already dead leader Li Bing-hook to public disgrace. It is clear that where such things were demanded, Point 7 of the above treaty was absolutely essential. . . .

In 1895, Russia extended her possessions in China still farther, and flirted with Korea; England took for herself Port Hamilton, an island South of Korea.

In 1884–1885, China was forced to fight against France which had stolen the whole southern part of Cochin-China. In July 1885, China signed the peace, promised not to interfere in the relations between France and Annam and paid a large indemnity.

In July 1886, Burma finally passed into English hands and in 1890 China was forced to recognize England's protectorate over the Himalayan state of Tsikim. (*Loc.* cit., p. 227.)

In 1894, the Sino-Japanese war broke out. The German imperialists were happy that the killing of two missionaries offered them a pretext: they threatened China with a war and thereupon received Kiaochow on a 99-year lease. *Kiaochow for the heads of two missionaries.* The German imperialists would not be averse to making such an advantageous deal every month. In 1899, Italy too attempted to squeeze something out for herself, but China had the strength to show her the door.

The imperialist Powers not only expropriated China, not only continued to regard her as an object of imperialist raids, but in addition they intervened in the *domestic* affairs of China, playing a counterrevolutionary role and supporting the Chinese reaction. There are ample instances of this.

At the beginning of the Fifties, an insurrectionary movement began in China which became known under the name of Taiping. This movement, which bore a somewhat religious character (it recalled the movement of the Anabaptists), was directed at the same time against the ruling Chinese dynasty. The movement continued to gain adherents and was borne from town to town. A regular state of war existed between the troops of the dynasty and the Taipings. The dynasty was preparing a most sanguinary defeat of the rebels. The troops of the imperialist Powers, however, deemed it their duty to support this bloody work. An especially sorry role was played by the soldiers of the noble Great Power, France, in the dispersal of the rebels from Shanghai in 1855. After they had surrendered, 1,700 rebels were executed, with the cooperation of the Great Powers. As reward, France demanded and received an extension of her settlements.

Russia also took part in the repression of the Chinese uprising of 1858—as equivalent of her Amur undertakings.

But the Taiping movement lasted into the Sixties. The troops which had remained loyal to the Chinese government, found it increasingly difficult to put an end to the movement. The Chinese reaction found itself compelled ever more frequently to appeal to the European Great Powers. And they came gladly to its aid—naturally, not without corresponding "compensations." In 1862, the English and French troops undertook to "purge" the 60-kilometer zone around Shanghai of the rebels. In February 1862, the French incorporated 900 soldiers, the English 1,000 into the Chinese regiments lead by Li Hung-chang. Together with him, they fought the rebels.

The tradition of this "counterrevolutionary" policy of the Great Powers in China was continued by imperialist Germany during the Chinese Revolution of 1911. In his book, officially marked for recognition by the German authorities, Schuler narrates that in the North of China, Tsingtao offered protection to all the highly-placed officials and the nobility who were able to save their lives and their possessions in this sure shelter. Curiously enough, the author complains that during the uprising the revolutionary Chinese press constantly fanned the hatred against the Germans because of their "alleged" support of the dynasty with weapons, munitions, *etc.*

Can one wonder after all this that the hatred of the European Powers is great in China? Can it be maintained—without hypocrisy—that Europe was forced to answer the outbreaks of Chinese fanaticism with "defensive wars"?

In 1899, the Ta Tin Tin (Society of the Great Knife) arose in China. In 1900, the secret league of the "Great Fist" (the English called the members of this society Boxers) arose which set itself the aim of fighting the Europeans and driving them out of China. There were excesses. The Chinese attacked the European consuls, killed, for example, the German consul von Ketteler, *etc.* Thereupon the European governments sent troops to China, which committed cruelties in comparison with which the deeds of the Boxers looked like innocent child's play.

But what caused the Boxer movement? The fact that the imperialists of all countries fell upon China like a pack of hungry wolves.

In 1894, China conducted a war against Japan over Korea. The Japanese triumphed and dictated the peace to the Chinese in Shimonoseki. The European imperialists promptly interfered in the affair. The spoils of their Japanese companion left them no rest. After the Peace of Shimonoseki, Japan was allotted Formosa, Port Arthur and a billion in indemnity. Korea was to become independent. Russia, France and Germany united against Japan. To throw sand in the eyes, it was stated that the intervention was caused by the declaration of independence of Northern China. In reality, both Russia and Germany felt only the lust for booty.

In Germany too imperialism had raised its head. Germany decided to lay claim to Kiaochow. . . : On May 4, 1895, Japan was forced to return Port Arthur and Liaotung to China. For this "friendly service" the four Great Powers were rewarded as follows: Germany received Kiaochow on a 99-year lease, and it was taken over by the Japanese in 1914. Russia received Port Arthur on a 35-year lease, England "leased" Weihaiwei, France Kwang Chu-wan.[7]

Thus was China divided and plundered by the European imperialists. Naturally this caused a just indignation among the Chinese people, which adopted desperate methods in its defense from the robbers. No honest person can contend that the European governments conducted a just war of defense in 1900 during the Boxer war. And the fact that the consuls of the European governments were attacked by the Chinese, alters nothing of the facts.

The island of Cuba

Wars conducted by peoples against imperialists upon whom they are dependent, are *just wars of defense*. Imperialist wars against colonial peoples are *unjust wars of aggression*. Wars that the imperialists fight among themselves have

7. Only the poor Austrian bourgeoisie failed at that time to squeeze anything out of China. Austria was then occupied by other things. All her attention was directed at carrying out the policy of Count Andrassy. Austria was thinking only of conquests in the Balkans. But the German-Austrian bourgeoisie is bitterly angry to this day because Austria did not then exploit the opportunity to plunder China. See, e.g., Professor Otto Hoetzsch, *Österreich-Ungarn und der Krieg* (Austria-Hungary and the war), 1915, p. 19.

the aim of dividing or re-dividing slaves and are therefore to be condemned; neither of the two sides is conducting a "just war of defense."

Let us consider as an illustration of the last case the war of Spain against the Island of Cuba and the war of America against Spain for the Island of Cuba.

The Island of Cuba was from times immemorial oppressed by Spain. In 1868–1878, a series of uprisings took place on the Island of Cuba. The Island was granted the same autonomy that all Spanish provinces possess. Beginning with 1881, Cuba sent 30 deputies and 14 senators to the Spanish Cortes. In 1888, slavery was abolished. In 1895, a new uprising broke out in Cuba; war began against Spain. Spain mobilized an army of 200,000 men which distinguished itself by inhuman cruelty. In spite of this Spain could get nowhere. Then America intervened in the situation.

For the North American imperialists it was a question of preparing the United States for participation in the struggle for the Pacific Ocean coasts. In addition, the Americans had sunk large sums of money into various enterprises in Cuba. Above all, the large reserves of tobacco, coffee, sugar, etc., in Cuba, the Philippines and Puerto Rico had long ago made the Americans restless. On April 23, 1898 Spain received an ultimatum from the President of the United States, McKinley. War breaks out between America and Spain. America triumphed and took from Spain (by the Paris Treaty of December 10, 1898) Cuba, the Philippines and Puerto Rico. The Monroe Doctrine[8] won and with it

8. The Monroe Doctrine is the doctrine of a President of the United States: North America must not permit any Power to have any possessions in the vicinity of the American coasts.

the moneybags of the American imperialists.

Although America proclaimed everywhere that it was fighting for liberty and independence, it now refused to grant the Philippines freedom. In 1900–1901, uprisings broke out intermittently in the Philippines and were suppressed by the Americans with the bloodiest means. Cuba obtained her autonomy and a republican constitution in 1901; whereas the Philippines were permitted to convene a National Assembly only in 1907, and all its decisions must first be confirmed by America.

Now the question is: Who is the aggressor party here, who the defender? Who conducted a just war and who an unjust? The answer is clear: Both parties, both the Spanish and the American imperialists, conducted the unjust war of two slaveholders for the possession of slaves. It would be ridiculous to examine *which of them* was aggressor and which defender. Only the *third* party conducted a just war of defense—the oppressed peoples of Cuba and the Philippines who fought for liberty and independence—against the Spanish and American slaveholders.

Morocco

In the ten years between 1895 and 1905 we see five great imperialist wars: the war between China and Japan for Korea in 1895, the war between America and Spain for Cuba in 1898, the war between England and the Boers for the diamond fields of Transvaal in 1899, the war between all Europe and China in 1900, because the Great Powers wanted to impose their railroads on China and enrich themselves at China's expense, and finally the war between Russia and Japan for the right to exploit Manchuria in 1904.

All these bloody wars did not bring the victors any particular territorial expansion: Manchuria continued to remain with China, China formally retained her independence, South Africa constitutes a politically autonomous state, Cuba becomes an "independent" republic. In spite of this, however, the victors nevertheless carried off their spoils: railroads, loans, customs duties, concessions, etc., became the possessions of the imperialists of that "fatherland" which bought its victory with streams of blood.

A second typically imperialist conflict was the one over Morocco, which even before 1914 almost led to a world war.

The industrial race between German and English capital forced imperialist England to seek an alliance with her old foe, France. In 1903 Edward VII paid a visit to France. What was the real cause of this visit? At that time that German-French syndicate was almost concluded. The German imperialists sought a *rapprochement* to the French and were prepared to "cede" a part of the Bagdad Railway. The Germans needed French capital. The German-French syndicate was founded. Arthur von Gwinner, director of the Deutsche Bank, was named President. For Vice-President, Vernes, colleague of the Rothschilds in the Compagnie du Nord and the Compagnie du Midi, member of the Council of the Union Parisiènne Bank and the Banque Ottomane, member of the Salonica-Constantinople Railroad Company, etc. Behind M. Vernes stood Rouvier & Co.

Edward VII appeared in Paris as the agent of the English imperialist bourgeoisie, in order to prevent the Franco-German syndicate. He succeeded, and paid with Morocco. The French imperialists renounced all claims to Egypt and left it to the English, receiving from the latter—Morocco. *Egypt for Morocco, Morocco for Egypt!*

This machination was presented to the "people" as an "Entente cordiale" (a "hearty alliance" in which it was not so much the heart that played a rôle as the purse).

Because the French imperialists abandoned all cooperation with the German imperialists, the English imperialists left the former the monopoly over the railroads, the ports, telegraphic system, public works, *etc.,* of Morocco.

The German imperialists, however, began brandishing their bayonets. They threatened to kindle a world war unless they received their share of Morocco. The conference in Algeciras found itself compelled to make certain concessions to the German imperialists. A certain percentage of the Moroccan loans was allotted to them and a sufficient sphere of influence for the import of capital, etc., guaranteed.

Although a peace is thus concluded, it is not of long duration. Europe is only a hair's-breadth removed from a world war. Both the German and the French and English imperialists want this war. It is postponed, but only because Germany is not finished with her naval armaments, the French decide upon 3-years' military service, etc. War may break out any day. Even then all the belligerents would have shouted that they had been attacked, that they are conducting a defensive war, etc. But in reality it would have become only an imperialist war, a war of a few cliques of finance capital for the not yet divided spoils.

Tripoli

Or let us take the Tripolitan war of 1911, which may be considered, along with the Turkish Balkan wars of 1912–1913, as the overture to the World War of 1914–1916. This war is a classic example of how deceptive and useless the criterion of the defensive war can be.

In September 1911, Italy quite unexpectedly sent Turkey an ultimatum: Italy has displayed till now—in case you did not know it—a most unusual patience and moderation, but Turkey absolutely refused to consider the "legitimate Italian interests" in Tripoli. Hence "Italy finds itself compelled" to occupy Tripoli. Turkey had not yet found the time to reply to this ultimatum when, on September 30, 1911, the bombardment of the forts of Tripoli was begun by the Italians.

This war too was of course declared to be a "just" war by the Italian imperialists. The whole apparatus at the disposal of bourgeois dominion was set in motion in order to evoke a patriotic spirit among the Italian people. And not without success. A genuine enthusiasm and spirit of enterprise gripped the whole Italian people who rallied unanimously around its king and his government. Even the larger part of the socialists (of the social-*reformists,* to be more accurate; Bissolati & Co. were expelled from the Italian Socialist party for this re-learning to the point of social-chauvinism) did not stand aloof from this enthusiasm and were ready for self-sacrifice. This is how the well-known historian of German foreign policy, Count Reventlow, describes the state of things in Italy at the beginning of the war for Tripoli.

And what was the actual meaning of the Tripolitan war, what was the real foundation of this whole affair?

The war was purely imperialistic, and the whole conflict was closely bound up with the race of two competing imperialist trusts.

From the moment when the *rapprochement* between England and France, directed at Germany, became noticeable, England began to feed Italy with promises. Right after Fashoda [1898 colonial dispute in East Africa between Paris and London], England promised Italy Tripoli. Now France was also prepared, for the pain it caused Italy in seizing Tunis, to "cede" Tripoli to Italy in the name of the "solidarity of the peoples of Romanic culture." In 1899 and in 1902, England and France formally gave Italy a note for Tripoli. For the success of their imperialist trust, they had to distract Italy from the Triple Alliance at any price. To this end, the Italian imperialists had somehow to be bribed. They paid—as usual—with others' possessions. Tripoli belonged neither to France nor to England. France had cast her eye upon it only because it lay in the vicinity of her own possessions.

After the "Entente cordiale" between the imperialists of England and France (1904), the Italian imperialists thought they already had Tripoli in their pockets. The "Entente cordiale", however, was, as we see, concluded under the motto: Egypt for Morocco. Expanded, the motto read: *For Egypt—Morocco, for Morocco—Tripoli.*

After the conference in Algeciras (1906), at which Italy, in appreciation for promised Tripoli, already openly supported England and France against her "ally", Germany, the imperialists of Italy were of the opinion that they had "honestly" earned Tripoli and considered themselves the masters of this colony.

When Italy declared war upon Turkey in 1911 because of Tripoli, the situation became a most difficult one for Germany. For Italy and Turkey were officially Germany's allies. To come out against Italy meant for Germany, first, to push Italy still further to the Triple Entente, and secondly, it would immediately provoke a world war for which Germany was not yet sufficiently armed. To come out against Turkey meant to drive the Turkish "ally" into England's arms, for the Turks had become convinced that Germany was unable to defend them and that their fate rested entirely in England's hands. A most difficult situation. Imperialist Germany squirmed like an eel and finally enacted the comedy of neutrality. At this price, Germany bought the continued existence of the Triple Alliance with Italy's participation—after Italy had taken Tripoli from the Turks.

The war for Tripoli was, as the reader sees, a link in the chain of imperialist conflicts. Turkey concluded peace with Italy at Lausanne on October 18, 1912, at a time when a new war had already begun in the Balkans. Here too the imperialist Great Powers were the stage-managers. The knot became ever more complicated until the inevitable occurred in 1914.

The Tripolitan war was a *typical* imperialist conflict, produced by the imperialist lust which has branded the whole epoch.

Now the question is: How far could the socialists and democrats get in these cases with the old criterion of defensive and aggressive wars? Italy was the aggressor. Did we therefore have to sympathize with the other party, recognize that Turkey was conducting a "just" war? In that case we would have been nothing but a plaything in the hands of German imperialism! Take the part of Italy? Then we would have become a tool of the other imperialist trust! Imperialist Italy stood with one foot in the camp of the Triple Entente, with the other in the camp of the Triple Alliance. The Italian imperialists stretched out their right hand to the imperialists of England and France, but continued with their left to hold the hand of the German imperialists. *Who then was defending himself, who was the aggressor?*

It was only an episode in a whole chain of imperialist policy of two trusts of states, *both* of which attacked the weaker and the unarmed, *both* of which divided the world and plundered whole continents. Only the national uprisings of the native population, directed at both imperialist coalitions, could be characterized as "just". Of the two coalitions, however, neither conducted a just war. The theory of the defensive war is—when applied to this war—senseless, a hollow phrase. In reality it serves only the duping of the peoples by their imperialist governments, which have transferred the ideology of the national liberation wars to an entirely different era. . . .

That is how things stand with all the conflicts and wars of the imperialist period. In the collisions of the imperialist cliques of all these countries, there cannot be, from the historical standpoint, an aggressor party and a defender party. *All* of them attack those peoples whom they single out as their booty. All of them seek in imperialism their salvation from the socialist danger.

That is why it would be absurd to apply the criterion of "just" wars of defense to the imperialist wars of the Great Powers.

Colonial conquests since the 1870s—wars that materialized and wars that didn't

Let us consider the most important events in the field of colonial conquest since the '70s of the Nineteenth century.

Since 1870, England has enriched itself in Asia with the following territories: Beluchistan, Burma, Cyprus, British North Borneo, Wei-hai-wei. The Straits Settlements were extended. In 1899, the protectorate of Koweit was taken over, the Sinai Peninsula was conquered, *etc.*

In Australia, England won the southeastern part of New Guinea, a part of the Solomon and the Tonia Islands.

In Africa: Egypt, the Egyptian Sudan with Nyanda, British East Africa, British Somali, Zanzibar; in South Africa, the two Boer republics, Rhodesia, British Central Africa; in West Africa, Nigeria, *etc.*

France conquered: Tonkin, Annam, Leos, Tunis, Madagascar, parts of the Sahara, of the Sudan, of the Ivory Coast territories in Dahomey, on the Somali coast, *etc.*

Germany carried off since 1884 (the official beginning of the German colonial policy): Cameroon, Togo, German Southwest Africa, German East Africa, New Guinea, a whole series of islands (Kaiser Wilhelm Land, Bismarck Archipelago, Caroline Islands, *etc.*).

Russia seized possession of Urga (in China) in 1870, of Kulchu in 1871, of Fergana in 1870, and then of Manchuria; finally, it has been pursuing its latest policy in Persia. . .

We have mentioned only the four Great Powers. But Japan too, since 1874, began its imperialist policy with the expedition against Formosa.

At the beginning of the Twentieth century, a few years brought about three sharp conflicts over Morocco, two over Balkan affairs. And each time European peace hung by a thread.

We present here an incomplete table of the wars conducted since 1870:

1870–1871, the German-French war.
1873–1879, Holland's war upon the Sultan in Sumatra.

1876, Serbia and Montenegro against Turkey.
1877–1878, the Russo-Turkish war.
1879, three English armies invade Afghanistan (concessions are made to England).
1883–1885, France against China (over Tonkin).
1885, Serbian-Bulgarian war (the Serbs are defeated at Slirnitza, Peace of Bucharest on March 3, 1886).
1885, Russia against Afghanistan ("victory" of General Komarov).
1893, war of the French and the conquest of Dahomey (Guinea).
1894, Japan against China over Korea (Japan wins).
1895, Spain against the Island of Cuba.
1896, Italy against Menelik (the Abyssinian war; Italy defeated).
1897, Greco-Turkish war (defeat of the Greeks; the Isle of Crete obtains autonomy in 1898).
1898, Spanish-American war (over Cuba; Spain defeated).
1899–1900, England's war against the Boers.
1900, war of the European Powers against China (Boxer war).
1904, England against Tibet (victory of England).
1904–1905, Germany against the Hereros.
1904–1905, Russo-Japanese war.
1911–1912, Italy against Turkey (over Tripoli).
1912, war of the Slavic Balkan peoples against Turkey.
1913, Serbia and Greece against Bulgaria.
1914, outbreak of the World War.

If these wars are analyzed, it is seen that most of them were of a purely imperialistic nature. Before us lies a segment of entirely new wars which are quite different from the national wars of the former epoch. Their causes are different. Their social content is different. They are the expression of a different stage of development of capitalism.

Of the same character are the majority of those conflicts in recent times which were resolved without war. The famous pacifist, Professor Fried, tried to make a list of prevented wars. In the period between 1904 and 1916, he enumerated 17 such wars that did not reach the point of outbreak. They include the following conflicts:

1. Hull incident, 1904 (conflict between England and Russia).
2. Moroccan conflict, 1905 (conflict between Germany and France).
3. Separation of Norway from Sweden, 1905.
4. Conflict between Japan and the United States, 1907.
5. Moroccan conflict, 1908 (France against Germany).
6. The Casablanca incident, 1908 (Germany against France).
7. Annexation of Bosnia and Herzegovina.
8. Austria against Turkey, 1908.
9. Bulgaria against Turkey, 1908.
10. Turkey against Greece, 1908 (over the Isle of Crete).
11. Japan-China, 1909 (over the Manchurian Railway).
12. Bolivia-Peru-Argentine, 1909.
13. United States-Chile, 1909.

14. Russia-Japan, 1909 (conflict over Manchuria).
15. Greece-Turkey, 1910 (Crete).
16. Chile-Peru, 1910.
17. Ecuador-Peru, 1910.

We thus see lying before us a whole period of imperialist conflicts and imperialist wars.

A few words on the savagery of modern colonial policy

The German imperialists began their colonial policy later than the others. Their first steps in this field were made almost at the beginning of the Twentieth century. And yet: how much blood and filth, how much violence and cruelty are on their heads!

Their whole colonial policy, from start to finish, is *one* crime. How incredible do their "treaties" sound which they conclude with the natives while stealing their land! "We, the undersigned independent [!] kings and army chiefs of Cameroon, cede our possessions to Herren Eduard Schmidt and Johann Voss, representatives of the firm of G. Wermann," reads one such treaty. In place of their signatures, 23 Negroes ("independent kings"), since they could not write, make the sign of the cross. . . The other part of Cameroon was sold to the same firm of Wermann for 150 tons of rum!

English and French capitalists acted the same way only a short time ago in India. Whoever is on the spot first, whoever hangs out his national flag first, is the master. . .

And then the cruelties and robberies of the servants of German imperialism against the population of the colonies!

Whippings are the lightest penalty in the Cameroons. During the uprising in Cameroon, hundreds of Negroes were tied together on the orders of the German officials, Leist and Wehlau, and left in the hot sun-rays until they died of thirst. The scum of German militarism is sent into the colonies, hence the unheard-of cruelties. Women are lashed with rods in the presence of their husbands, whole settlements are burned to the ground and left to die of hunger. Shooting is resorted to on every occasion. At the beginning of the Herero uprising, this tribe numbered about 100,000 persons. According to official statistics, there were only 21,699 left on January 1, 1913: 7,071 men, 9,209 women and 5,420 children.

In 1905, a new uprising broke out in East Africa. The introduction of forced labor, inhuman taxes and constant executions, provoked the uprising of the Matmuba tribe. The German soldiers gave free rein to their lust for pillage. In 1913, the German Colonial Office declared in an official report that 20,000 natives lost their lives at the time. The German Professor Schilling, however, asserted that no less than 150,000 natives were killed during the uprising. Villages were burned, the crop destroyed. Many weakened natives became the prey of lions. The lions were satiated with human flesh at that time. . .

We are writing about the cruelty of the German imperialists. But cruelty is not a characteristic of the German imperialists alone. Let us recall what reached the public about the policy of English imperialism in India, of the policy of the Belgian government in the Belgian Congo, of the French policy in the French colonies! Let us mention only this, that according to the calculations of Sir William Diglys, in the period from 1850 to 1870 in India, 5,000,000 persons died of *hunger,* and in the period from 1875 to 1900, some 26,000,000.[9] Let us add that in 1896, 2,000,000 Indians died of the plague. Let us recall further that the former English Viceroy of India, Lord Curzon, estimated the average annual income of an inhabitant of British India at $6.50. And all this frightfulness is produced mainly because England exports the largest part of the Indian crop (hence the starvation), and that taxes and imposts are placed mainly upon the agricultural population (about 80% of all the taxes)!

Recently, an interesting booklet on English customs in India was written by the former American Secretary of State, William Bryan, who collected personal experiences. This booklet, which appeared in the Indian language, was immediately confiscated by the English government. The American periodical, *Coast Seaman,* produces some data which are taken from this booklet. The tax burden in India is relatively twice as heavy as in England. Mortality, which was 2.4% in 1882–1884, was 3% in 1892–1894, and is now 3.4%. Starvation takes on terrifying dimensions. "England boasts of having brought peace to India, in reality it has brought death to millions of persons in India. . . It sucks the sap of life from India by means of robberies which are justified by law." Thus writes not some "agitator", not even some "German", but a man who occupied a high post in the friendly American government.

In 16 years, 8,000,000 persons died of the plague in India; the land tax amounts to 65%; the average earnings of

9. For details, see, e.g., Dr. Herm. v. Staden, *Indien im Weltkrieg* (India in the world war), Stuttgart, 1915.

an Indian amount to 10 cents. But England gets a yearly income of $166,000,000 from India. Thus writes the committee of the Indian Revolutionary Party in an appeal made public in San Francisco in 1916.

Let us recall the "international expeditions", which, the famous American politician, Morgan Schuster (who was a Persian minister in 1911), wrote in his book in 1912, made all literate Europe indignant—a book that bears the eloquent title, *The Strangling of Persia.*[10]

The true motives of imperialist war

In 1909, the well-known English monthly, *The United Service Institution,* published the excellent prize-awarded treatise of a high English naval officer. In this treatise, we find the following noteworthy lines:

> We [England] undertake no war out of any sentimental reasons. I doubt if this has happened even once. War is the product of commercial conflicts; the aim of war—to impose upon the enemy those economic conditions one considers necessary for oneself. We utilize all possible pretexts for war, but their actual causes are always questions of trade. Whether defense or the necessity of a strategic position is alleged as the cause of war, whether treaties must be violated or similar reasons play a part—in the long run everything has its origin in commercial interests.

---

10. W. Morgan Schuster, ex-Treasurer-General of Persia, *The Strangling of Persia, A Record of European Diplomacy and Oriental Intrigue,* London and Leipzig. 1912.

> For the simple but decisive reason that trade is our heart's blood.

What is, is said here clearly and openly: "We imperialists (this of course also applies to the German imperialists) seize upon any pretext, we speak of defense, of violated treaties, *etc.* But the essential is one thing: the money-bag, the interests of the capitalists."

That is the pure truth. That's what imperialist wars are. Outward causes and pretexts may seem credible. One is "defending" himself, another is fighting nobly for the independence of a country, a third is defending the interests of "civilization", purely out of idealism, against "Russian barbarians".

In reality, however, all fight for the interests of a handful of magnates of finance capital.

What has the criterion of defensive wars to do with all this?

> It is extremely easy to distinguish defense and attack in words, but extremely difficult in practise to establish exactly who is the aggressor and who the defender. In almost all the wars of recent decades, as in former times, both sides considered themselves the attacked. (J. J. Ruedorffer, *Grundzüge der Weltpolitik in der Gegenwart* [Main features of world politics today], p. 218)
>
> By and large, the instrument of arbitration courts serves only to avert the outbreak of *unwanted* wars. . . (*Loc. cit.*, p. 167.)
>
> Whoever considers the history of the colonial expansion of the Great European Powers in recent

> decades . . . will find without trouble that all the wars of modern times in which the Great European Powers participated were, if not contrived by the interests of capital, at least initiated by them. (*Loc. cit.,* p. 157.)

These are the valuable admissions of the well-known German imperialist, Ruedorffer. So far as candor is concerned, they are not inferior to the above-mentioned declarations of the decorated English author.

Even the bourgeois-democratic pacifists have rightly appraised the true value of the assertions of all imperialist governments: “We” are the attacked, “they” are the attackers. In the international organ of these pacifists, *La Voix de l'Humanité,* January 5, 1916, we find the following table, drawn up not without humor:

> *Every belligerent state contends:*
> 1. That it is conducting a defensive war and is fighting for the just cause.
> 2. That it is conducting a fight for the freedom and civilization of all peoples.
> 3. That it is striving for a lasting peace.
> 4. That it is bending all efforts and will fight until the enemy has been conclusively beaten.
> 5. That it will be the victor, beyond a doubt.
> 6. That it is forging ahead victoriously and has only slight losses to record.
> 7. That the bombs of its aviators hit only the military institutions of the enemy and always with great success.
> 8. That its aviators and its artillery are far better

than the aviators and artillery of the enemy.

9. That at this very moment it is planning great measures which promise absolute success.
10. That the good Lord is on its side.

And every belligerent state further contends:

1. That the enemy wanted the war and was preparing for it long ago.
2. That the enemy began the war and attacked "us".
3. That the enemy is conducting a war of conquest and wants to dominate the world.
4. That the enemy is trampling underfoot the rights of the people.
5. That the enemy has violated the neutrality of the small states and threatens the neutrality of other small states.
6. That the enemy is conducting the war with barbarous means.
7. That the enemy uses dum-dum bullets.
8. That the enemy is misusing the Red Cross.
9. That the enemy mistreats prisoners.
10. That the enemy violates women, murders and plunders.
11. That the military courts of the enemy are a mockery of the law.
12. That the enemy kills prisoners.
13. That the enemy bombards open cities, kills women and children, but does not do "us" the slightest military damage thereby.
14. That the attack of the enemy is always nipped in the bud or else is beaten back with great losses for the enemy.

15. That the enemy is using gas bombs.
16. That the enemy is a pirate on the high seas.
17. That the enemy is needlessly preventing neutral trade.
18. That the reports of the enemy are lies through and through, and calumnies to boot.
19. That the enemy is trying to influence the neutrals by means of lies, threats and bribery.
20. That the enemy is egging the neutral states on to war—to their greatest misfortune.
21. That the enemy is suffering from a lack of money, rising living costs, industrial crises.
22. That the war loans of the enemy are subscribed only by means of deception.
23. That epidemics are ravaging the enemy.
24. That strikes and domestic disturbances are the rule in the land of the enemy.
25. That the enemy's ministers and generals are resigning.
26. That the enemy is war-weary.[11]

This list could be extended further. . . .

If the wide masses of the people could read the newspapers of all countries, they would see that the ruling classes say the same thing everywhere, they would be convinced that the bourgeoisie employs the same methods everywhere, the same "technique" for the deception of "its" people. But the masses of the people read—if they read at all—only the

11. *La Voix de l'Humanité*, No. 58, 1916. Prominent politicians of France, England and other countries contribute to the editing of this periodical.

press of "their" bourgeoisie and of "their" social-chauvinists, who only parrot the wisdom of their homeland bourgeoisie. And it is noteworthy that the same arguments, the same "technique" function in all the belligerent countries. There is but one thing left for the bourgeois and social-chauvinistic writers to do: in place of the name of one fatherland, to put the name of another, *e.g.*, Germany in place of Russia, and their goal is attained.

Some concluding remarks

The stage of the *military armament* of a given country may serve as one of the important factors for an objective estimation of which side is the aggressor from the *diplomatic* standpoint and which side the defender. Tell me who is better prepared militarily for the war, and I will tell you who it is that wanted the war at the given moment, who brought it about! Naturally, it may happen that this or that government has overrated its war preparedness, or that it is compelled, *in spite of* insufficient armament, to begin the war—for example, for reasons of domestic policy, *etc.* But all other conditions being equal, the thesis just put forward is absolutely applicable.

Back in the earliest days, there were great disputes over the question of which side was the aggressor and which the defender. Most decisive is the outcome of the war itself, victory or defeat in the war. History usually characterizes as the aggressor the one who has *triumphed.* The war of the Huns against the Visigoths in the 70s of the Fourth century may serve as a classic example from early times. Most historians agree that in 373 the Visigoths attacked. The Huns, however, are known in history as "Huns" because they proved to be the stronger in the course of the war.

Book after book has been written on the diplomatic history of the war of 1914–1916. The social-chauvinists respect dates and the contents of the dispatches of this or that diplomat on the eve of the war as exhaustive arguments. We are less interested in the question. The contents of the White, Yellow, Gray and other books, which contain fragments of the diplomatic negotiations, have of course a great significance for the appraisal of the system of modern diplomacy. But a serious importance for judging the character of the war of 1914–1916 and for establishing the socialist tactic in this war, is not contained in them. It is very likely that public opinion will consider that side the aggressor which carries off the final victory.

Such a judgment would not be an absolutely arbitrary one. Both belligerent sides would like to win; but the victory depends mainly upon the degree of military armament. The one that was better prepared militarily, has more objective prospects for winning, and all other conditions being equal, had more cause to undertake the war; and can therefore—again, all other conditions being equal—be considered as the directly aggressive side.

On the basis of her military armament, Prussia was able to undertake a war of aggression against France in 1870. Bismarck's machinations lead Napoleon III to declare war first. But when it later appeared that France was not at all prepared militarily, whereas Prussia was excellently armed, down to the last button on her soldiers' coats—this was the best objective proof that Prussia, *at that moment,* had wanted the war.

The degree of military armament still has the same importance today. At the beginning of the war of 1914, Germany was again best prepared for the war; and once more this gives one the right to think that *at that moment* Germany wanted the war.

But this has absolutely no importance for the position of the working class towards the wars of our epoch in general, and towards the war of 1914 in particular.

We have seen that even in the epoch of the national wars, the question of who attacked first was not decisive for democracy. In our present epoch, however, defensive wars in the old sense of the word have become altogether impossible.

Twenty-five years ago, Wilhelm Liebknecht, who had the epoch of the national wars in mind, spoke of a "just" war, one in which he admitted the participation of the social democrats. A quarter of a century later, Plekhanov digs up these words in order to be able to say: That's right, we too are for a "just" war.

By referring to Liebknecht's words about a "just" war, Plekhanov facilitates a rectification of his false contention. For in reality, what does Plekhanov's juggling with the criterion of defensive war consist of? Of this, that he mixes up two epochs—the epochs of the national wars and the epoch of the imperialist wars.

Can "just" wars in general still take place in the imperialist epoch?

Yes, but only in two cases. The first case would be the war of a proletariat which has triumphed in some country, and which defends socialism against other states which represent the capitalist régime. The second—a war of China, India or similar countries which are oppressed by the imperialism of other lands and are fighting for their independence *against* these imperialist Powers.

The replacement of one epoch by the other appears most crassly in Italy. In 1859, we saw there a typically national war. In 1859 it was a question of the emancipation of Italy from the Austrian yoke, of Italian unification, in which *the whole people, the whole of democracy,* was interested. Austria was the oppressor, Italy the oppressed.

In 1859, shortly before the war, we see a man like N. A. Dobrolyubov stigmatize Austria by having her say the following words:

> We, your Masters, are inexpressibly outraged
> That you rebel-folk disturb us with your rising! . . .
> What? For forty years, without once giving way,
> We shielded all the world from your blunders! . . .
> Upon you we lavished all that we possessed:
> Spies, new hangmen, garrisons and jails.
> E'en our speech, our customs, the law and the tribunal—
> And what is your thanks for Austria's faithful aid?
> For shame! What would you that we grant you more?
> Why can we not, as heretofore, in noblest concord live?
> Or mayhap our soldiers there are still too few for you?
> Or else maybe the police we have you think is ill-advised?
> Why, swiftly do we move! The remedy is instant,
> A regiment we'll gladly quarter in every town and hamlet. . .

And now? Now things look quite different. Now Italy fights against Turkey for Tripoli, against Austria for Albania, Dalmatia, Istria. Can one still speak today of a just defensive war of Italy?

A just war *between* imperialist governments is impossible, just as impossible as a "just" struggle between several thieves for the division of their loot. *Every war—except for the two cases named—is, in our time, an absolutely "dishonorable" war.*

Nor can it be otherwise, so long as we apply a terminology suited for *one* epoch to one that is entirely different. There can now be no "just" wars between the Great European Powers which pursue imperialist policy. The Triple Alliance and the Triple Entente were the two important Power groupings, decisive for all of European policy. And these two groupings arose, lived and acted under the sign of imperialism, where, as Kautsky rightly observes, one plays the aggressor today, the other tomorrow, and then back again.

If those socialists who till now considered the criterion of defensive war correct could learn from history, they would have to say now: "Up to now we held to this criterion and—we now experience the collapse of the Second International, an unheard-of, unprecedented disgrace. *Anything but the repetition of August* 4, 1914! Anything but the repetition of this shame, in which, by applying the criterion of defensive war, we become traitors to the proletariat, agents of the bourgeoisie!"

And whatever the fate of the Workers' International may be—one thing can be said today with assurance: the theory of defensive war must be buried for all honest socialists. The experience of 1914 has buried it.

Can there be a more convincing, a more grewsome lesson than the one given by the war of 1914–1916? A theory which lead to the collapse of the International during such events can no longer be defended.

Where have the "defense of the Fatherland" and the theory of defensive war lead us? To the policy of August 4, to the Südekums of all countries, to complete collapse!

During the war, so long as the passions still rage, one can, if he is stubborn, continue to adhere to the criterion of the defensive war: "We are defending ourselves, we are in the right!" But once the war ends, and one is forced to draw the balance, everyone who thinks honestly will have to give up this criterion.

Could one speak, in the "just" national wars of the earlier epoch, of the struggle of the bourgeoisie against the proletariat, which put the socialist overturn on the order of the day? No, there could be no question of that. For the conditions were not yet ripe for socialism, the proletariat had not yet gathered itself together, everywhere, as a class. In the imperialist wars, however, the struggle against the labor movement is one of the main tasks of the imperialist bourgeoisie.

To characterize an imperialist war as "just" is possible only for an agent of the bourgeoisie. Now, however, this is, unfortunately, done also by such people as call themselves socialists.

"We are conducting a just war!" cry Südekum and—Hindenburg. "No, it is we who are conducting the just war," answer Plekhanov and Thomas. . . .

The criterion of defensive war has long ago become obsolete. If it had not happened long before the war of 1914, this war would have buried it. What has this war showed? Who appealed to the criterion of defensive war? Everyone and no one. Everyone—for to justify their piratical policy, the imperialists of every country seized upon it, the diplomats and governments of all the peoples, the deceivers of the European press, regardless of their language. No one—

for no one really took the criterion seriously.

And then the International! Could the criterion of defensive war save it from collapse? All the parties, including the official social-chauvinistic ones, assure us that they are holding strictly to the criterion of defensive war. Germans, Frenchmen, Italians—all contend that they are observing the principle of defensive war. Who among them is right? Everyone and no one. For the principle, in and by itself, is no longer valid. For the proletariat, however, it has now lead to the collapse of the Second International.

There was a time when even Plekhanov knew that the abstract criterion of defensive war is not worth much. In August 1905 he wrote:

> Just as dogmatic is the viewpoint that we socialists may sympathize only with "defensive wars". Such a viewpoint is correct only from the standpoint of the conservative *suum cuique.* The international proletariat which consistently defends its standpoint, must be in sympathy with every war which—*regardless whether it is a war of defense or aggression*—can remove an important obstacle on the road of the socialist revolution.[12]

Plekhanov's terminology is not very clear. He makes no distinction between the defensive war in historical respects and the defensive war in diplomatic respects. In any case, however, he perceives that the theory of defensive war is

---

12. See, *Social-Democratic Diary,* No. 2, "Patriotism and Socialism." A reply to a questionnaire of the editors of the periodical *La Vie Socialiste.*

inadequate and false. Defensive or aggressive war, it makes no difference, says Plekhanov. Only a dogmatist can think that "defense" or "attack" is decisive for us. For us socialists the problem is somewhat different. Decisive for us are the interests of the social revolution.

> The class struggle assumes an acute revolutionary character, it overturns the old conceptions handed down by earlier generations; and moreover where the oppressed class convinces itself that its interests are identical with the interests of the oppressed classes of other countries, but are opposed to the interests of the ruling classes of its own country, the *concept of the Fatherland* loses in large measure its former allure. (*Plekhanov.*)

For decades the Marxists labored to deprive the bourgeois idea of the Fatherland of its attractive power, they repeatedly showed the workers how similar in form was the position of the oppressed classes in the various Fatherlands. But now, when the first imperialist war has begun, when the imperialists utilize the idea of the Fatherland in order to dupe the workers of all countries—now the former Marxist Plekhanov also glorifies the idea of the Fatherland! What an enormous turn-about-face! From Marx and Engels to Heine and Südekum—that is the path trod by the former Marxists who now render homage to social-chauvinism.

Frederick the Great once said that when monarchs wanted war, they began it and then commissioned some zealous jurist to prove that right is on their side.

When we see how the Plekhanovs and Südekums of all

countries are acting now, the expression of Frederick the Great can be modified in the following way: When the imperialists want a war, they begin it and then commission a zealous social-chauvinist to prove that right is on their side.

Gregory Zinoviev
HARTENSTEIN, SWITZERLAND
AUGUST 4, 1916

$12

$15

$20

Three books to be read as one . . .

about building a party that's working class in program, composition, and action. One that recognizes, in word and deed, the most revolutionary fact of our time . . .

. . . that working people have the power to create a different world as we act together to defend our own class interests—not those of the privileged classes who exploit our labor, not of those who fear us as "deplorables," or just plain "trash."

As we advance along a revolutionary course toward workers power, we will transform ourselves and awaken to our own worth. Also in Spanish, French, Greek.

Special Offer!
All three $30

The Turn to Industry and *Tribunes of the People and the Trade Unions* $20

Either book plus *Malcolm X, Black Liberation, and the Road to Workers Power* $25

PATHFINDERPRESS.COM

THE BOLSHEVIKS AND THE FIGHT AGAINST NATIONAL OPPRESSION

Lenin's Final Fight

Speeches and Writings, 1922–23

V.I. LENIN

In 1922 and 1923, V.I. Lenin, central leader of the world's first socialist revolution, waged what was to be his last political battle—one that was lost following his death. At stake was whether that revolution, and the international communist movement it led, would remain on the revolutionary proletarian course that brought workers and peasants to power in October 1917. $17. Also in Spanish, Farsi, Greek.

Workers of the World and Oppressed Peoples, Unite!

Proceedings and Documents of the Second Congress, 1920

The debate among delegates from 37 countries takes up key questions of working-class strategy and program and offers a vivid portrait of social struggles in the era of the October revolution. 2 vol. set. $45

Questions of National Policy and Proletarian Internationalism

V.I. LENIN

Why the fight of oppressed nations for self-determination is decisive in the worldwide proletarian struggle to take and hold power. Why workers and farmers in imperialist countries have a deep class interest in championing this right. $16

To See the Dawn

Baku, 1920—First Congress of the Peoples of the East

How can peasants and workers in the colonial world achieve freedom from imperialist exploitation? By what means can working people overcome divisions incited by their national ruling classes and act together for their common class interests? These questions were addressed by 2,000 delegates to the 1920 Congress of the Peoples of the East. $17

The Revolution Betrayed

What Is the Soviet Union and Where Is It Going?

LEON TROTSKY

In 1917 workers and peasants of Russia were the motor force for one of the deepest revolutions in history. Yet within ten years a political counterrevolution by a privileged social layer, whose chief spokesperson was Joseph Stalin, was being consolidated. The classic study of the Soviet workers state and its degeneration. $17. Also in Spanish, Farsi, Greek.

The First Ten Years of American Communism

Report of a Participant

JAMES P. CANNON

A founding leader of the communist movement in the US tells the story of the early years of the effort to build a proletarian party emulating the Bolshevik leadership of the October 1917 revolution in Russia. Among other things, Cannon writes, "Everything new and progressive on the Negro question came from Moscow, after the Bolshevik revolution and as a result of it." $17

PATHFINDERPRESS.COM

FROM PATHFINDER

The Low Point of Labor Resistance Is Behind Us

The Socialist Workers Party Looks Forward

JACK BARNES, MARY-ALICE WATERS
STEVE CLARK

The global order imposed by Washington in the aftermath of its victory in World War II is shattering. A long retreat by the working class and unions has come to an end. More and more workers of all ages, skin colors, and both sexes are saying, "Enough is enough!" This book highlights opportunities ahead for building a mass proletarian party able to lead the struggle to end capitalist rule, opening a future for humanity. $10. Also in Spanish and French.

In Defense of the US Working Class

MARY-ALICE WATERS

Drawing on the fighting traditions of the oppressed and exploited of all colors and national origins, in 2018 tens of thousands of teachers and other working people in West Virginia, Oklahoma, and other states waged victorious strikes. They fought for dignity and respect for themselves, their families, and for all working people. $7. Also in Spanish, French, Farsi, Greek.

U.S. Imperialism Has Lost the Cold War

JACK BARNES

The collapse of regimes across Eastern Europe and the USSR claiming to be communist did not mean workers and farmers there had been crushed. In today's sharpening capitalist conflicts and wars, these toilers are joining working people the world over in the class struggle against exploitation. In *New International* no. 11. $14. Also in Spanish, French, Farsi, Greek.

Are They Rich Because They're Smart?

Class, Privilege, and Learning under Capitalism

JACK BARNES

In battles forced on us by the capitalists, workers will begin to transform our attitudes toward life, work, and each other. We'll discover our worth, denied by the rulers and upper middle classes who insist they're rich because they're smart. We'll learn in struggle what we're capable of becoming. $10. Also in Spanish, French, Farsi, Arabic.

The Teamster Series

FARRELL DOBBS

Four books on the strikes, organizing drives, and political campaigns that transformed the Teamsters across the Midwest in the 1930s into a militant industrial union movement. Written by Farrell Dobbs, the general organizer of these Teamster battles and leader of the Socialist Workers Party.

A tool for workers seeking to use union power in every workplace and advance the fight for an independent labor party. $16 each, series $50. Also in Spanish. Teamster Rebellion is also available in French, Farsi, Greek.

The Communist Manifesto

KARL MARX AND FREDERICK ENGELS

Communism, say the founding leaders of the revolutionary workers movement, is not a set of ideas or preconceived "principles" but workers' line of march to power, springing from a "movement going on under our very eyes." $5. Also in Spanish, French, Farsi, Arabic.

EXPAND YOUR REVOLUTIONARY LIBRARY

Labor, Nature, and the Evolution of Humanity

The Long View of History

FREDERICK ENGELS, KARL MARX
GEORGE NOVACK
MARY-ALICE WATERS

Without understanding that social labor, transforming nature, has driven humanity's evolution for millions of years, working people are unable to see beyond the capitalist epoch of class exploitation that warps all human relations, ideas, and values. Only the revolutionary conquest of state power by the working class can open the door to a world free of capitalist exploitation, degradation of nature, subjugation of women, racism, and war. A world built on human solidarity. A socialist world. $12. Also in Spanish and French.

50 Years of Covert Operations in the US

Washington's Political Police and the American Working Class

LARRY SEIGLE, FARRELL DOBBS, STEVE CLARK

How class-conscious workers have fought against the drive to build the "national security" state essential to maintaining capitalist rule. $10. Also in Spanish and Farsi.

Cuba and the Coming American Revolution

JACK BARNES

This is a book about the struggles of working people in the imperialist heartland, the youth attracted to them, and the example set by the Cuban people that revolution is not only necessary—it can be made. It is about the class struggle in the US, where the revolutionary capacities of workers and farmers are today as utterly discounted by the ruling powers as were those of the Cuban toilers. And just as wrongly. $10. Also in Spanish, French, Farsi.

Malcolm X Talks to Young People

"The young generation of whites, Blacks, browns, whatever else—you're living at a time of revolution," said Malcolm in 1964. "And I for one will join with anyone, I don't care what color you are, as long as you want to change this miserable condition that exists on this earth." Four talks and an interview in the last months of Malcolm's life. $12. Also in Spanish, French, Farsi, Greek.

Capitalism and the Transformation of Africa

Reports from Equatorial Guinea

MARY-ALICE WATERS, MARTÍN KOPPEL

Describes how, as Equatorial Guinea is pulled into the world market, both a capitalist class and a working class are being born. Also documents the work of volunteer Cuban health-care workers there—an expression of the living example of Cuba's socialist revolution. $10. Also in Spanish and Farsi.

Pathfinder Press **accessible e-books** for the blind, those with low vision, or other challenges reading print books

For a list of current accessible titles, go to: pathfinderpress.com/collections/books-for-the-blind.

Visit bookshare.org for information on how to sign up.

FURTHER READING

The Jewish Question

A Marxist Interpretation

ABRAM LEON

The battle against reactionary forces aiming to exterminate the Jews remains central to world politics, as shown by the genocidal October 2023 pogrom in Israel. Why is Jew-hatred still raising its ugly head? What are its class roots? Why, as Abram Leon explains, is there no solution "independent of the world proletarian revolution?" Revised translation, new introduction, and 40 pages of illustrations and maps. $17. Also in Spanish and French.

Is Socialist Revolution in the US Possible?

A Necessary Debate among Working People

MARY-ALICE WATERS

Fighting for a society only working people can create, it is our own capacities we will discover. And along that course we will answer the question posed here with a resounding "Yes." Possible but not inevitable. That depends on us. $7. Also in Spanish, French, Farsi.

The Clintons' Anti-Working-Class Record

Why Washington Fears Working People

JACK BARNES

What working people need to know about the profit-driven course of Democrats and Republicans alike over the last three decades. And the political awakening of workers seeking to understand and resist the capitalist rulers' assaults. $10. Also in Spanish, French, Farsi, Greek.

CUBA'S SOCIALIST REVOLUTION

Women in Cuba: The Making of a Revolution within the Revolution

VILMA ESPÍN
ASELA DE LOS SANTOS
YOLANDA FERRER

The integration of women in the ranks and leadership of the Cuban Revolution was intertwined with the proletarian course of the leadership of the revolution from the start. This is the story of that revolution and how it transformed the women and men who made it. $17. Also in Spanish, Farsi, Greek.

The First and Second Declarations of Havana

Nowhere are the questions of revolutionary strategy that today confront men and women on the front lines of struggles in the Americas addressed with greater truthfulness and clarity than in these uncompromising indictments of imperialist plunder and "the exploitation of man by man." Adopted by million-strong assemblies of the Cuban people in 1960 and 1962. $10. Also in Spanish, French, Farsi, Arabic, Greek.

Our History Is Still Being Written

The Story of Three Chinese Cuban Generals in the Cuban Revolution

ARMANDO CHOY, GUSTAVO CHUI
MOISÉS SÍO WONG, MARY-ALICE WATERS

"What was the key measure to uproot discrimination against Chinese and blacks in Cuba? It was the socialist revolution itself." New edition sheds light on Chinese Cubans' involvement in Cuba's internationalist course, including in Africa and Latin America. $15. Also in Spanish, French, Farsi, Greek, Chinese.